Explore
Yorkshire by Car

2. The North York Moors

by Alan A. Falconer

Dalesman Books
1979

£1.25

The Dalesman Publishing Company Ltd.,
Clapham (via Lancaster), North Yorkshire.

First published 1972
(as "Motoring on the North York Moors")

This edition 1979

ISBN: 0 85206 549 3

Volume 1 covers The Yorkshire Dales

Printed in Great Britain by Galava Printing Co. Ltd.,
Hallam Road, Nelson, Lancashire.

Contents

The front cover photograph of Hutton-le-Hole is by Tom Parker.
The new Parkway (A171) and new stretches of the A19 are omitted
from the maps on pages 10, 13, 34 and 37.

This book is based on articles which originally appeared in the
Middlesbrough Evening Gazette, now the *Teesside Evening Gazette.*

Introduction

THIS book is divided into two parts. The first section, "Places to Visit", describes some of the most interesting areas and features of the North York Moors National Park. It should form a valuable introduction to motorists who have only a scant knowledge of the area, at the same time refreshing the memories of those who are more familiar with this glorious stretch of upland country. There are several recommended walks from the car, while the accompanying sketch maps should suggest numerous possible itineraries.

The second section, "Some Detailed Routes", is for motorists who prefer to follow a prescribed run rather than plan their own journeys. Most of the routes are based on Teesside, the nearest conurbation to the North York Moors, but as the great majority of them are circular they can readily be adapted so as to start and finish at any suitable point. The maps accompanying the first section can be used as a basis for route finding, but for detailed navigation it is strongly recommended that a finely detailed map be purchased. One that is excellent for the purpose is the one-inch Ordnance Survey tourist map, "The North York Moors".

Part One:

Places to Visit

Cottages at Hovingham (W. A. Grainger)

Coastal Woodlands

THE Cleveland coast has a climate all its own. Even on hot calm days in high summer there is still the danger that a sea breeze may set in about midday and blanket the coast in drenching mist. Fortunately the effects of such a sea breeze are not felt far inland—rarely more than a mile or two. It is possible, therefore, to pack up the picnic things and seek shelter in the wooded valleys which radiate from all our favourite beaches.

There are roughly three types of woodland classified according to their path pattern: rough woodland with paths alongside the streams; rough woodland with cross-paths linking the farms and hamlets on either side of the valley; and well maintained "private" woods and gardens with broad gravel or macadam pathways. The first type is found along the banks of the streams entering the sea at Saltburn and Skinningrove. The woods are long established and the paths fairly well trodden by folk from the former mining towns round about.

The second type is found near Staithes. Several steeply banked rifts penetrate far into the hinterland reaching almost to the main moor road near Scaling reservoir. The paths in these woods cross the series of valleys to link the farms and hamlets on the ridges. There is far more undergrowth in these woods and keepers do not appreciate excited dogs alarming the pheasants at any time of the year. To take advantage of the public rights of way in these woods alongside Roxby and Scaling Becks the motorist will need to find parking space on the narrow grass verges of the lanes such as Ridge Lane which link the Whitby coast road (A174) with the moor road (A171).

Thirdly, there are more formal woodlands with well maintained gravel walks such as the Italian Gardens at Saltburn and the delight-ful woods around Mulgrave Castle near Sandsend. Here there are large car parks near the beach. There are paths on both sides of the streams so that visitors may plan a short stroll up one side and return by an alternative route.

The Mulgrave woods are private woodlands but are at the time of writing open to the public on Wednesdays, Saturdays and Sundays. The rhododendrons are brilliant in early summer and for the antiquarian there are two ancient castles half hidden on the narrow ridge between Sandsend Beck and East Row Beck. Another "private" wood gay with rhododendron and with good broad drives is at

7

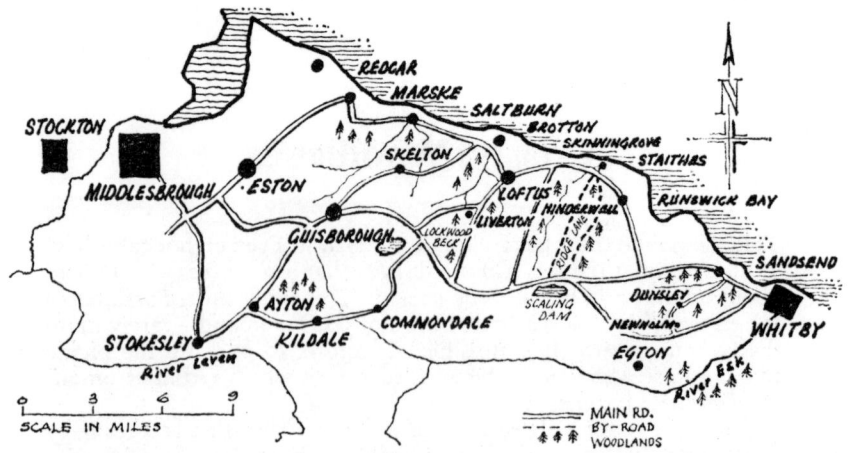

Kildale below Captain Cook's monument. The narrow gorge through which the Leven flows at this point is most impressive — very similar to the "Rift" of Riftswood at the western end of Saltburn's Italian Gardens. Almost all our local valleys show these features, massive rock walls usually below a delightful waterfall; and you can see such views near Roxby and Scaling Mills, and below Liverton Mill in the Kilton Woods (where there is a pleasant picnic spot just above the mill on the wide grass verges of the winding road from Lockwood Beck to Liverton).

The National Park warden and the Forestry Commission have had occasion to warn the public of the fire danger in North Yorkshire. In spite of our clouds and mists we are after all one of the driest areas of England — our rainfall is only just over 20 inches per year compared with 60 in some holiday areas of the west. The dead bracken and the dried grasses among the undergrowth can easily be ignited by a carelessly dropped match or cigarette end. Needless to say, picnic fires are definitely prohibited in all forestry areas. While on the subject of picnics I must appeal to motorists to take ALL litter home. Plastic bags may harm animals: those dainty paper napkins and tissues should be stuffed in the car ashtray, not in the nearest hedgerow after use.

Some of the by-roads I mention are not marked on the normal tourist maps. I strongly recommend any motorist who wants to explore the byways of Cleveland to invest in the Ordnance Survey one-inch sheet of the North York Moors National Park. This not only shows delightful narrow lanes through the wooded areas, such as those linking Newholm, Dunsley, Lythe and Sandsend, but also indicates the public paths through the woods and fields. Many of

8

these have been signposted since the Countryside Commission authorised councils to spend adequate sums on footpaths. You cannot fail to notice the new light green and white finger posts pointing the quiet ways leading off the noisy motor roads.

I assume that all Teesside motorists must have travelled the A174 and the A171 to and from Whitby. How many have fumed at the bottleneck at Guisborough on Sunday evenings? As an alternative try the delightful return route through Kildale and come back by Ayton or Stokesley. This way leaves the moor road above Lockwood Beck reservoir; at White Cross you turn right to Commondale and pass through Kildale village. It is at the foot of the hill in this little hamlet that you should turn off to the north along a road "unsuitable for motors" if you wish to visit the ravine of the Leven referred to earlier.

Finally, a word of caution to those venturing for the first time into the sylvan glades—there is a risk of mud, even in dry weather. This is partly due to tractors ploughing deep ruts as they drag felled timber along the forestry rides and partly due to the increasing use of the paths by ponies from local riding schools. This warning does not of course apply to the Saltburn Gardens or the well maintained Mulgrave paths.

Bilsdale—Newgate Bank and Chop Gate

BILSDALE, one of the main arteries through the North York Moors, has car parks at Newgate Bank and Chop Gate.

In one sense I was rather sorry to see a car park provided in this tiny hamlet, since few motorists will see much to interest them hereabouts. Fifty years ago there were still a few old folk in the village who could recall the boisterous times when there were three pubs to satisfy the mighty thirst of the numerous jet miners who crowded into the village on pay nights. The present general store was then the Tiger Inn, and the village lock-up was close by. It was in the care of a constable elected by the local farmers, and whose insignia of office was a stout staff and a pair of handcuffs. Below the Tiger was the Buck, where the beer was brewed, and across the River Seph at Seave Green was the Fox and Hounds. Only the Buck remains of these three and the cricket field lies behind it. Chapel Yat ran two cricket teams in its heyday and they were photographed, but probably did not play, in top hats.

9

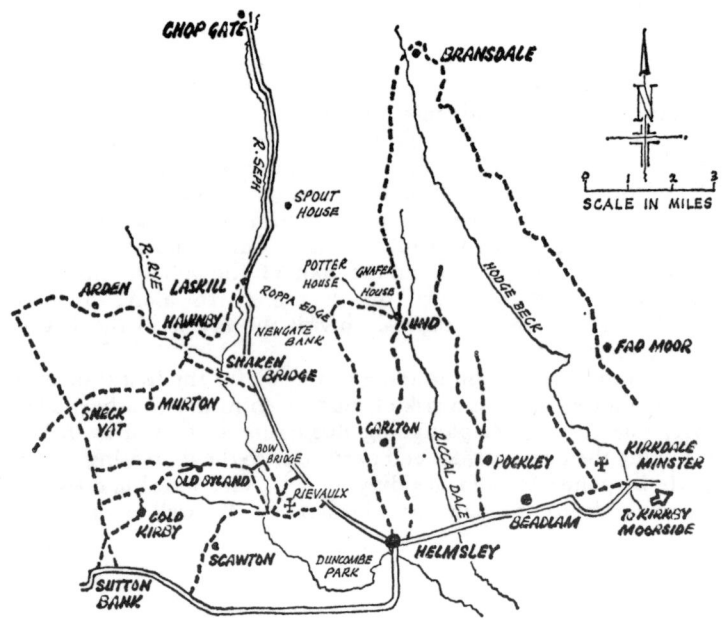

Today there is little to delay the passing motorist in Bilsdale. At Spout House, that is the Sun Inn, you may see a rather unusual single-storey Tudor house with its mullioned windows and thatched roof. The car park at the south end of Bilsdale at Newgate Bank Top attracts hundreds of visitors and with very good reason. There is, of course, one of the finest prospects in Yorkshire — particularly looking north up the dale to the shapely hills of the Cleveland range, and westwards to the green tablelands and dark wooded ravines of the Hambleton Hills.

It is a pity that two or three easy excursions across the River Seph towards Hawnby, which were popular with the Caravan Club in years gone by, are no longer possible because the footbridges have been swept away. Those readers who use the one-inch tourist map of the National Park should note that the red-dotted footpaths to Grimes Holme and Easterside are therefore no longer available. By a rather anomalous contrast, this same official document fails to mark a most attractive, well-used path through the Hag woods on the left bank of the Rye. This takes you into Rievaulx village. If you are fond of walking there is a gated path, which is marked on the ordnance map, on the right bank linking Ashberry Farm near Rievaulx Bridge with Shaken Bridge Farm just below Newgate Bank car park. This stroll up and down Ryedale would fill a long summer afternoon, but by using the narrow road over Bow Bridge you can halve the distance — but then you do not of course see Rievaulx!

The sketch map marks the little by-roads which link the east bank of the Seph and the Rye with the villages and the old Drovers' Road on the Hambleton Hills. Although the Drovers' Road continues northwards towards Chequers Inn near Osmotherley it is not metalled for cars beyond Sneck Yat near Murton. Around Old Byland, Scawton and Cold Kirby there are metalled rides through the forestry plantations — but they are not available for motorists: this is because in many cases the Forestry Commission has merely leased the land for planting and the owners reserve their rights — particularly where there are fish or game.

To the east of Newgate Bank lies Riccaldale. This remote valley is not famous for its broad panorama or scenery on the grand scale. It is rather a treasure house for the miniaturist. The little green hairstreak moth, the dwarf chickweed wintergreen, the swarms of ants are perhaps the three features which make this valley so beloved by the naturalist. It is also famous as the home of the stream that flows uphill. The Carlton watercourse, built by the Duncombe estate surveyor Joseph Foord in 1759, appears to climb up the steep escarpment of Roppa Edge to supply Carlton and Helmsley with water from a spring on the moors northeast of Spout House.

There are two broad forestry roads into Riccaldale from Newgate Bank — one runs along the top and the other lies just below Roppa Edge. These two rides are linked by the narrow county council road running from Helmsley Church to Potter House at the head of Riccaldale. Potter House is an isolated farm, chiefly pasture land sheltered by the forested slopes. There was formerly, as the name implies, quite a thriving pottery close by; it provided a taste of gracious living for tenants on the Duncombe estates, who normally ate and drank from wooden platters and "leather-bottles". The York visitors with whom Riccaldale is specially popular approach by a road from a turning at the east end of Helmsley. This road goes through Carlton and drops down into the dale at Cowhouse Bank, where there is one of the "surprise views" so typical of these tributaries of the Rye and Derwent. There is rather a fine run around the head of Bransdale if you continue north from Cowhouse Bank through Lund. Then you can return via Fadmoor to Kirkbymoorside on the A170.

Most of the roads north from the A170 peter out after three or four miles. The farms and villages on the limestone overlooking the Vale of Pickering seem to have had no need for roads into the bleak Blackamoor further north. I show two or three of these lanes leading up to Pockley, Skiplam, Carlton and Potter House. There is a wealth of wonderful country on each side of most of these roads. There are rocky dry valleys which it is great fun for the kiddies to explore; they might even come across another Kirkdale Cave with the bones of a sabre toothed tiger and mammoth tusks dating back before the Ice Age.

I mark the quiet Minster, or church, of St. Gregory at Kirkdale; the access to this ancient church is reasonably well signposted but it is very narrow and parking space is very limited indeed. It is the kind of spot, perhaps, to be avoided at weekends, but it is a shrine that should not be left without pilgrims. The attraction lies partly in the remarkable beauty of its setting, white limestone against a screen of tall dark cypress. But the main point of interest is the 10th century sun-dial in the porch. The dial face is divided into the Saxon eight tides, not the Roman 12 hours. The lettering is remarkably fine and to many observers it certainly proves that our Anglo-Saxon ancestors seemed to have a fine culture and greater love of beauty than their Norman conquerors. One can only regret 1066 and all that!

Eskdale

IN 1840, White's Directory of the North Riding lamented the fact that almost one house in every four was standing empty in the area between Guisborough and Sleights—that is roughly the moorlands and tributary valleys of Eskdale. Good stonebuilt cottages were sold for as little as 30s. The Guisborough Union Workhouse had just been built to accommodate 250 persons, in contrast to West Cleveland's Stokesley Workhouse which had been enlarged to entertain only 60 guests.

As Mr. White predicted, the opening of the Quakers' railway to the port of Cleveland at Middlesbrough was followed by extensions of the railroad along the Esk Valley: the motor car has increased its accessibility. House property has now risen several thousand per cent; even if a tiny cottage does fall vacant, prices are prohibitive for all except those from the stockbroker belt or the executive class of industrial Teesside. Fortunately the weekend motorists and holiday visitors can enjoy the manifold attractions of Eskdale, whose natives are mounting a vigorous campaign against the intrusion of weekenders.

At no time of the year are the moorlands more colourful than in August. The pale purple patches of bell heather have been in bloom for almost a month but the smaller buds of the calluna vulgaris are only just beginning to burst into their full glory. You will see the dark purple-stained bird droppings on the roadside which are clear evidence that ripe bilberries can be found nearby. Youngsters should be shown how to distinguish bilberry from the

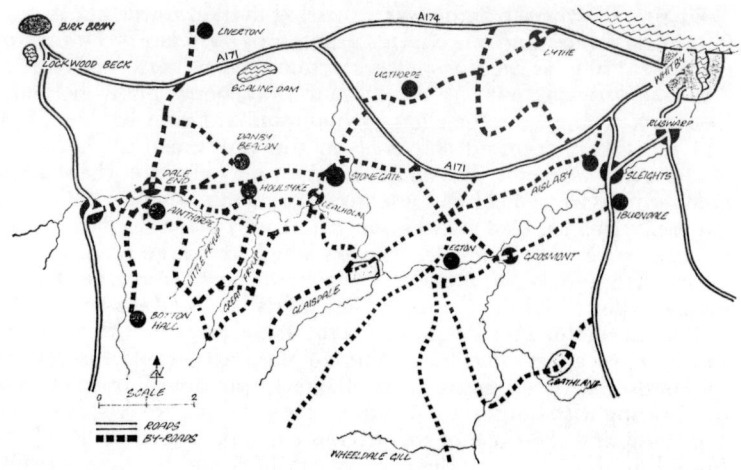

wild rosemary which often grows alongside it. The ripe bilberry has grey bloom on it, rather like black grapes; the rosemary is shiny. The bilberry is bell shaped and rather larger than the globular rosemary, which has a spiked bright green leaf, compared with the bilberry's oval, pink foliage.

Danby, a name which comprises six or seven scattered hamlets and townships, stands at the head of Eskdale just below the junction of Commondale Beck and Baysdale Beck with the infant Esk from Westerdale. The area was important in days long before the Romans crossed the Esk near Grosmont en route for their camp at Goldsborough. The ancient British tribes must have been at war: there are two long lines of entrenchments crowned with huge slabs of standing stone. These face each other across the Esk — one on Ings Moor north of Commondale, the other on Danby Rigg south of Ainthorpe. The Brus family later built its first stronghold on the mound overlooking the railway station and Esk bridge at Castleton. The square, fortified manor house in Little Fryupdale is a 14th century building associated with the Latimer family who inherited a third of the Brus lands on the failure of the Brus male line.

Less than a mile east of the Duke of Wellington at Danby End you will find the National Park Information Centre at Danby Lodge. Here there is excellent, supervised parking space and the film shows, guidewalks and lectures add to the attractions of the useful pamphlets and books on sale. The display of maps and pictures is most useful in helping to understand the main features of this most interesting dale.

Further down river Egton was a thriving market township; it held four annual fairs under a charter granted by William of Orange in the year 1700, as well as a weekly market for corn and cattle. All that survives today is the annual Gooseberry Show held the first week of August in the village schoolroom at Egton Bridge. More and more cars seem to converge on the tiny green at Lealholm Bridge every weekend. The children fish or play about in the shallow pools which are typical of these great sweeping bows or holmes in our local streams. Canon Atkinson noted with pride the beauties of the attractive steeply wooded ravines which converge on Lealholm from north and south. Stonegate Glen runs down from the Beacon ridge on the north side. Crunkley Glen starts below Great Fryupdale.

The Lealholm green is a sore sight for eyes after the weekend visitors have gone. The local binman naturally wants his rest at weekends and the three tiny litter baskets near Board Inn are soon overflowing with bottles, ice cream cartons and plastic crisp packets. The wind and the slope of the ground carry the overflow of lighter rubbish into the Esk and their traces can be found far downstream. There is only one real answer—"Take your litter home".

There are other spaces in and around Eskdale where opportunity to enjoy the sun, the air and the splendid scene is available. Birk Brow is perhaps the largest, but possibly the least attractive of the public car parks. Farther along new sections of the A171 there are laybys on the old road, above the enlarged and renovated Jolly Sailors Inn for instance. Just below the top of the moor, when you turn off the moor road from Danby village or the Beacon, there is parking space at Liverton Lane end. Here you may shelter from the breeze in the hollow Paddy Waddell Bridge. This is a reminder of the fierce competition of the early railway age when poor Patrick Waddell was building a railway from Guisborough towards the iron-stone of Grosmont, but the Battersby-Whitby line sponsored by the Peases won the legal battle for their rival project before the other line was completed and so the Station Hotel at Moorsholm became the Plough, and Paddy Waddell's cutting has become a picnic spot. A mile or two beyond the moor top, Scaling Dam has its attractions nowadays. Sailing is confined to members of the Scaling Sailing Club, but fishing is open to all permit holders and payment is made at the office on the site, where the county council is providing spacious parking and picnic facilities for the motorist. If you are no expert sailor you may still enjoy an hour's boating in the tea gardens by the roadside between Sleights and Ruswarp and finish off with a crab tea.

As the sketch shows you may wind your way from village to village along the Esk, following the signposts. Go warily along the narrow walled lanes and change gear early when you approach the steep sharp bends of the hills. Test your brakes if you have crossed the long, roughly cobbled ford on the gated road between Egton and

Grosmont on the south side of the Esk. The surface is smoother, the road wider on the north bank, but the views not nearly so attractive. If you want to get away from it all—try the Stape road from Egton Bridge to the forestry rides of Wheeldale Gill.

Rosedale's Old Railway

IT is one of the ironies of life that, after the motor car has caused the closure of so many railway lines, the derelict tracks and station yards should be used more by motorists than almost any other section of the community. At both seaside and country holiday spots, commodious station yards provide spacious car park facilities and I am thinking of Staithes and Aysgarth in particular. At one time there was a suggestion that disused rail tracks could afford some relief to our congested roads. The suggestions did not get much support—obviously most of the disused tracks were far too narrow. Furthermore they took such tortuous routes to avoid gradients that they sometimes trebled the distance the crow flies.

However, some of the old cinder and stone rail beds have been adapted to make wayfaring easier. The North York Moors National Park has utilised the rail track from Sandsend station to the old Kettleness tunnels as part of the Cleveland Way from Helmsley to Filey. This short section of the Coastal Path needs no nailed boots, maps or compass—any motoring party may walk along this pleasantly shaded railway cutting, sheltered from all the stormy winds that may be blowing. I always find railway embankments full of colourful and unexpected flowers. I remember observing, but not being able to identify, a patch of deep blue flowers, which could almost have been delphinium; they were on the old line on Warsett Hill, Huntcliff—another section of railway incorporated in the Cleveland Way. I suppose huge exotic poppies are the most noticeable of these railway flora, but at Sandsend there were masses of red valerian to offset the broom, the gorse and the clouds of blue harebells. Very soon it is hoped the old line from Whitby to Scarborough will be purchased by the new Scarborough Council.

The most useful old railway of all, however, especially to the motorist who wants a breath of moorland air without slogging up and down through tough, waist-high heather, is the former Rosedale Railway. This winds across the main watershed between the dales which run south to the Derwent and the Vale of Pickering. Several miles of it were dedicated as a public right of way by the late Earl of Feversham. Much of it is 1,000 feet above sea level and there are good prospects from several of its former embankments. As the

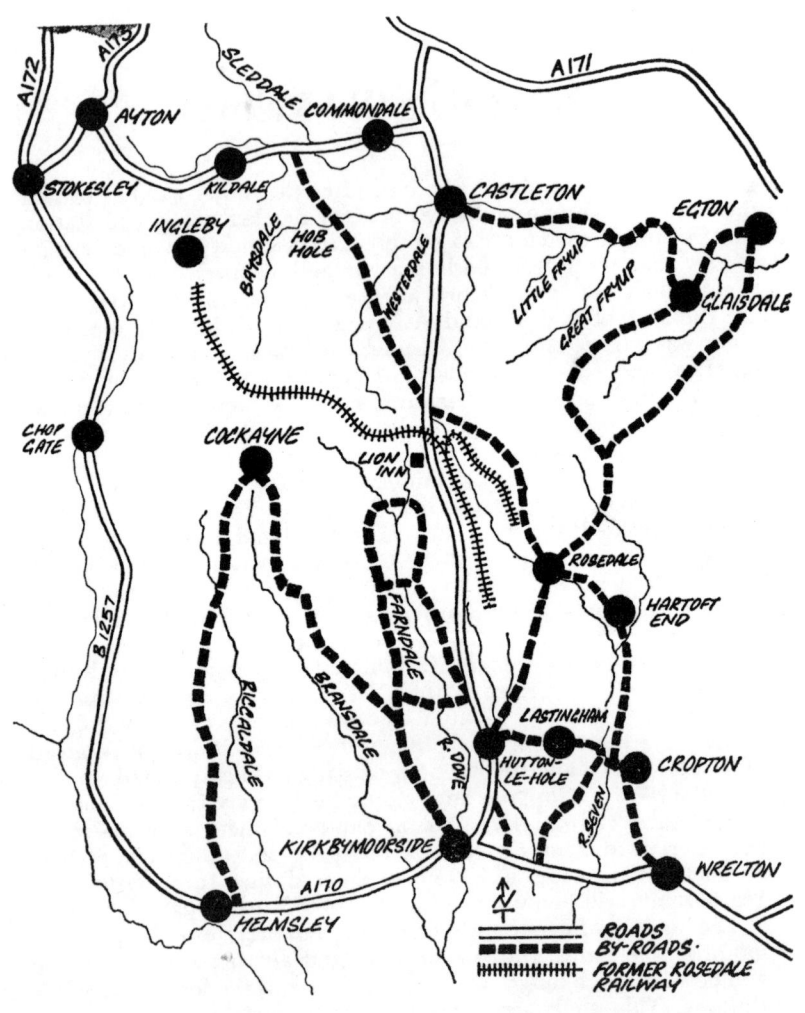

ROADS
BY-ROADS·
FORMER ROSEDALE
RAILWAY

map shows, the railway crosses the main road from Castleton to Kirkbymoorside just south of the Lion Inn on Blakey Rigg. It then runs along both sides of Rosedale Valley and every weekend dozens of motorists, particularly from the flats of Humberside, seek here the invigorating air of the high moorlands.

The smooth, grass-covered track around Rosedale is sufficiently high to command a wonderful view of the dale, but far enough below the ridge to escape the full force of the high winds so typical of the area. After carrying ore from Rosedale mines to Teesside and South Durham for 80 years, the Rosedale railway closed in 1929 when it became obvious that Cleveland's hard-won ironstone could not hold its own. Richer ores were much more easily acquired with mechanical shovels in shallow quarries or open cast workings in Northamptonshire.

There are some indications that the Romans made use of local ore and certainly the industry flourished in the early mediaeval times. Charters of the 12th century mention smithymen in Rosedale; they were permitted to cut down the great oak trees which used to cover the slopes of the dale and in return they delivered each week 16 stone of iron to the steward of the Abbot of St. Mary's, York. The mediaeval "bloomeries", or furnaces, were a mile or so south of Rosedale Abbey so it is not surprising that the Blacksmith's Arms at Hartoft End should be situated just across the River Seven opposite these older ironworks. As it took 40 massive trees to produce quite a modest lump of iron it is obvious why Rosedale is singularly bare of the woodlands that grow in so many of our local dales.

The area further south, however, offers a delightful contrast. The treelined roads around Hutton-le-Hole, Lastingham and Cropton sport fine blossom. The bushes bloom later and longer in this high country and under the shade of the dark pines of the Cropton forest I particularly liked the contrast of the pale, drooping laburnum and the glowing rhododendrons.

Lastingham and Hutton-le-Hole vie with each other as the prettiest of North York Moors villages. The church at Lastingham is one of the earliest of all Saxon stone buildings and one of Middlesbrough's more recent churches is named after St. Chad who was brother of the founder and first abbot. There is a tremendous fund of interest at Hutton-le-Hole where Ryedale Folk Museum offers a varied collection of relics of local history. The county council has provided excellent parking facilities on the north-east side of the village green. Both at Lastingham and Hutton there are excellent illustrated guides available and it would be unworthy and impossible to quote at length from these handy booklets. I would recommend, however, some exploration of this area even if your main object is to sample the sea at Scarborough or the golf at Ganton.

Vary the usual overcrowded route via the moor road (A171) or the Bilsdale — Helmsley — Pickering run (B1277 and A170). Go out by Ayton and Kildale and at the top of Kildale valley turn off to the right to Westerdale. This road has a water splash which can be fairly deep after heavy rain. Above Westerdale, at Ralph's Cross, you join the Castleton — Blakey Rigg road between Farndale and Rosedale and go through Hutton-le-Hole to join the A170 at Kirkbymoorside.

Return from the Vale of Pickering to Teesside by leaving the A170 at Wrelton for Cropton. Follow the signposts carefully on this winding tortuous way through Cropton, Lastingham and Hartoft End to Rosedale Abbey. Here you may go straight ahead through the village back to Ralph's Cross and Westerdale, or by climbing up the steep hill alongside the Milburn Arms you can use the roads along Glaisdale Rigg or Egton Rigg. These cross the Esk Valley to reach the A171 — the Whitby Moor road. The sketch map names several other little tributary valleys but most of them have no through road. Perhaps they may be all the better for that and offer a chance of peace and quiet.

The Hambletons

THIS run explores the western end of the Cleveland Hills and the charms of the Hambletons. The area is bounded by four good main roads — the newly completed A19 affords Durham and the West Riding rapid access to these attractive hills. The B1257 through Bilsdale skirts the eastern boundary of the area whilst along the south and north boundaries are the A170 and the A172, which link the A19 with the Bilsdale road.

While expecting readers to meander at leisure along the winding by-ways of the area, I must not fail to emphasise that the view of the long range of the Cleveland Hills from the A170 between the Tontine and Stokesley is a sight not to be missed on a fine summer's evening, so make your way back to Teesside this way whatever else you may decide to do. There are about half a dozen narrow lanes branching off the A19 into the foothills of the Hambletons. All the villages have dignified stone cottages with an amazing array of colour — plum blossom and clematis climbing the walls and masses of every imaginable bloom in the flower beds. The lanes wind amongst the curious rounded knolls, as at Kirby Knowle, and through some magnificent parklands around the manor houses which are a feature of the district.

There are four large car parks which I mark on my map: at Hasty Bank, Newgate Bank, Sutton Bank, and at Sheep Wash near

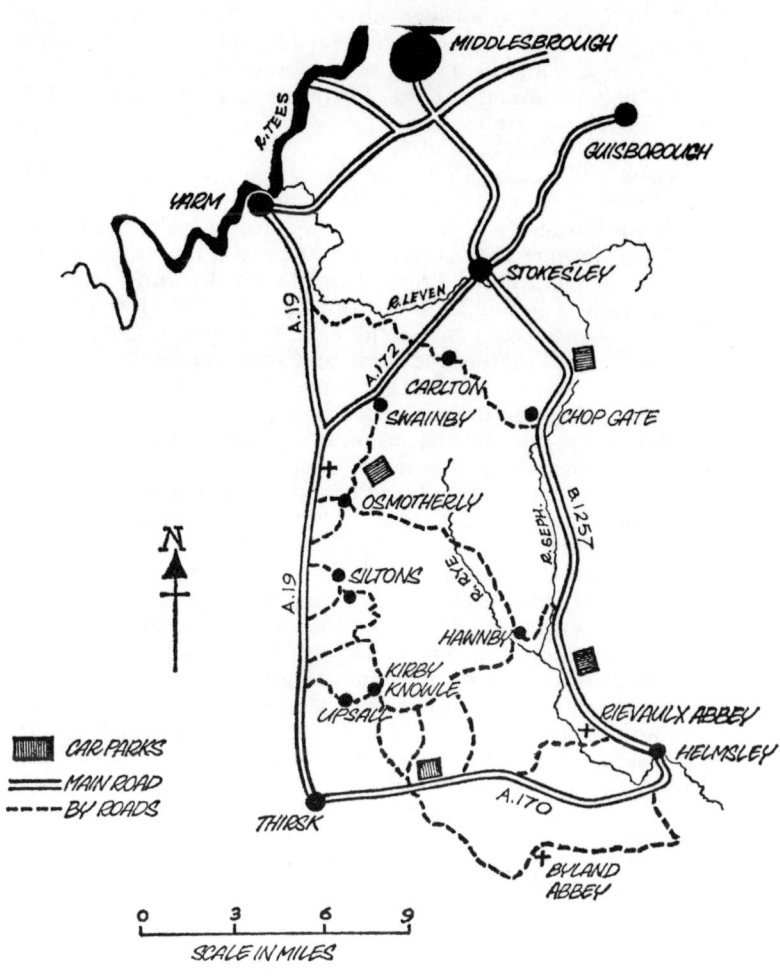

MIDDLESBROUGH

GUISBOROUGH

R. TEES

YARM

A.19

R. LEVEN

STOKESLEY

A.172

CARLTON

SWAINBY

CHOP GATE

OSMOTHERLY

B.1257

R. SEPH.

N

A.19

SILTONS

R. RYE

HAWNBY

KIRBY
KNOWLE

UPSALL

RIEVAULX ABBEY

HELMSLEY

A.170

THIRSK

BYLAND
ABBEY

CAR PARKS
MAIN ROAD
BY ROADS

0   3   6   9

SCALE IN MILES

19

Osmotherley. The area around Sutton Bank offers the widest variety of attractions for those who wish to leave their cars for a gentle stroll to watch more strenuous folk. There will be climbers risking the perilous ascent of Whitestone Cliff, heavily laden hikers en route from Helmsley to Scarborough on the Cleveland Way, and high above the aeronauts will be soaring in their gliders. Most exciting of all, perhaps, would be a glimpse of thoroughbreds at exercise on the Hambleton training gallops. There are also ponies from local riding schools churning up the woodland footpaths—don't, therefore, risk a walk in sandals.

The new Information Centre on the car park is a mine of useful knowledge on every aspect of the National Park.

Below the Sutton Bank car park the wooded slopes of the hillsides above Lake Gormire have been earmarked as a conservation area by the Yorkshire Naturalists' Trust. This part of the world has been, almost literally, a goldmine for botanists for more than a century. So many rare plants could be found here that orders came in for specimens from all parts of the world and greedy collectors have dug up so many of the rarer plants that many are now extinct. Pesticides and fertilisers have added to the destruction, so much so that even the common cowslip and the primrose are becoming scarcer each year—particularly the first named flower.

Most of us have heard that Dorothy and William Wordsworth took a walk from Thirsk to Scarborough and passed through this region, famed even then for its beauties. I consulted Dorothy's "Journal" but was more than disappointed. I knew that Edmund Bogg in the 1890s recorded more than 160 flowering plants and 200 different birds in his booklet on "The Charm of the Hambleton". Dorothy, strangely, mentions only one wild flower—the rose, and one song-bird—the thrush. Dorothy also remarked on the bright roofs of the houses, but said nothing of the deep beauty of Gormire, the legend of the white mare that leapt from the crag into the lake, nor the devil's footprint on the eminence of Hood Hill. I do not think much of Dorothy as a walking companion.

There is a little pamphlet available at the car park published for the Naturalists' Trust. The sketch map shows "Jennet's Well" at the north end of Whitestone Cliff, at the point where a bridle road through Thirlby linked Thirsk with the old cattle drovers' road across Black Hambleton. Local folk call this "Janette's" Well, and the assumption is that it was named after some forgotten beauty. The origin of the name is, however, much more utilitarian—a Jennet or Jenny was a riding horse. More than 1,500 of these were reared on the rich Hambleton pastures in former days, and this well was their only available water.

Goathland's Waterfalls

THERE was a time not so very long ago when our schoolchildren learned poetry instead of studying literature. From that dim past a couple of lines still stick in my memory and ever and anon keep on repeating themselves: "... books in the running brooks, sermons in stones and good in everything."

This phrase particularly comes to my mind whenever I am in the region of Robin Hood's Bay. It is here more clearly than anywhere else in North Yorkshire that the rocks tell the story of the Creation and the Flood: not in the words of the Old Testament or the legends of Ancient Greece, but in the more modern image of a strip cartoon, where images have replaced words in this non-literate age. It is at the southern end of Robin Hood's Bay that the earth's surface shows clear signs of a massive upheaval. A huge block of rocks was thrust upwards at Ravenscar and an equally massive block slid down and away from the Scar. Above these lie three series of layered sandstones laid down when the whole of the area was a vast delta — sometimes with reptiles and plants whose fossilised remains provided a poor quality coal. Between the deltaic periods deep seas covered the land and the remains of shellfish gave us our limestones.

It was of course the Ice Age which created the wonderful scenery of the area. The great glaciers from Shap Fell, the Cheviots and Scandinavia choked all the valleys with deep deposits of boulder clay; the older stream channels often disappeared. The flood waters of melting ice gouged out deep new gorges from the rocks. They are most impressive near Mallyan Spout and Falling Foss; thus the running brooks continue the sermon of the stones of Ravenscar. The huge fault which lifted up the Peak at Ravenscar also helped to create the impressive waterfalls which are to be found in the narrow valleys, a mile or two inland from the bay.

The nearest to Robin Hood's Bay is Falling Foss below the aptly named Midge Hall. The Forestry Commission has levelled two high-capacity car parks here and they have proved very popular — better known perhaps to West Yorkshire folk than to Teessiders. To reach the Falling Foss parks you must cross the Esk and approach the fall from the east side at a sharp corner of the Whitby-Scarborough road, the B1416, above the village of Sneaton. At this point the signposts indicate the alternative routes. Due south, through a double gate, takes you in a half circle across the open moor to the May Beck car park. The road south-west leads to a car park closer to Falling Foss just beyond the Yorkshire Naturalists' hostel at Newton Hall. There is also a narrow road north-west to Littlebeck village.

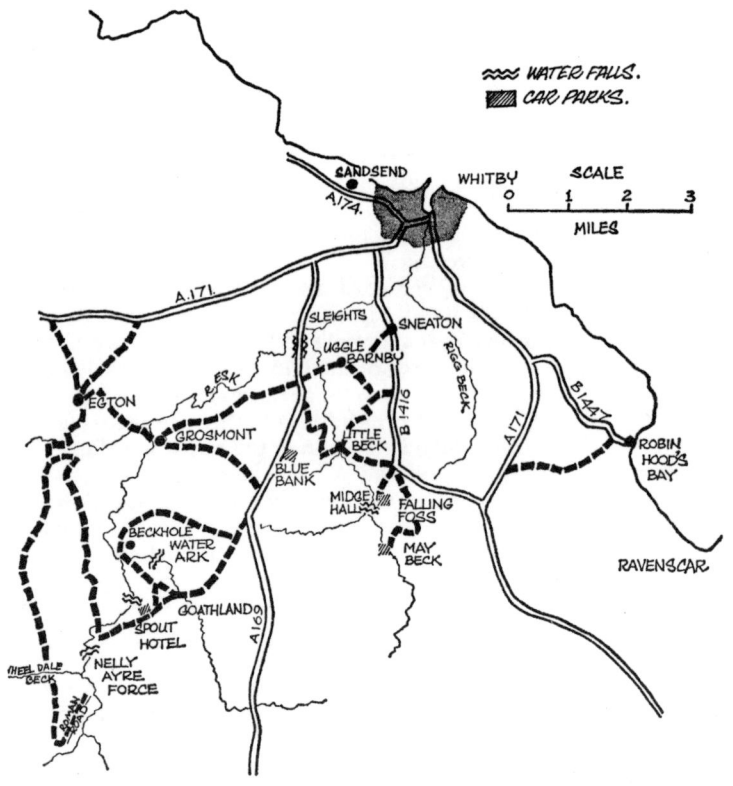

There is a supply of pamphlets available at each of these parks. Youngsters can get a lot of fun following the clearly marked trails through all the well-established woods hereabouts and at Midge Hall there is another chance to consider the sermons in stones as the Naturalists have arranged a simple display of some of the more important and easily recognisable rocks found in this area. The moorlands to the south of Falling Foss and the deep gorge of Newton Dale are not crossed by any road "suitable for motors". Accordingly, to get from the valley of the May Beck to the three falls near Goathland it is necessary to make a long detour.

It is an interesting run to work your way along Harwood Dale, leaving the Whitby-Scarborough road above Cloughton; then go through the Wykeham Forest to Pickering and so reach Goathland from the south. Teessiders, however, will normally approach Goathland from Sleights or Egton Bridge which lie just below the A171, the main moor road to Whitby from Teesside. I have introduced a map showing a small area—it supplies rather more detail than the usual motorists' road maps and it is based on Bartholomew's half-inch map of Yorkshire. Modern techniques of printing work miracles, but frequently the detail and the print is so fine that the naked eye can hardly read the print nor distinguish between paths, roads, contours and county boundaries. They certainly cannot be successfully read by the average back seat driver whilst travelling at 40 miles or more an hour. This sketch shows a road through Littlebeck linking the B1416 with the A169 which runs from Sleights to Pickering. This narrow road is one to be avoided at weekends at all costs. There really is not room for two cars to pass, especially on the steepest pitches (1 in 3) on the west side of Littlebeck.

At Goathland, it makes quite a challenging, but rewarding stroll to leave the car near the Mallyan Spout hotel and go down the signposted well-used path to see this graceful cascade. Then you retrace your steps and go above the woods before dropping back to Station House. This is now a delightful cream-washed cottage and a well-trimmed green, flat lawn hides the site of the old railway sidings at the foot of Goathland incline. This incline railway is shaded by tall trees and covered with a flowery carpet, in particular the pale candles of one of the orchids caught my eye, could it have been Orchis Maculta, spotted orchid? From this point follow the incline back to Goathland's broad village green with the commoners' sheep cropping the short grass.

By car, Beck Hole can be reached from the road junction near the prominent mound on the A169 which carries the stump of Lilla Cross, where a memorial tablet will give you all the details. This by-road forks near the end of the Cleveland Dyke quarries; the volcanic rock quarries here are a continuation of those at Cotham Stob, Great Ayton and Lonsdale. There are samples of their blue-grey basalt stone on display at Midge Hall. From the bridge at Beck Hole you may make a very adventurous way upstream to the twin falls of Thomasson Foss and Water Ark. They are, however, more easily approached if you park near the isolated hamlet of Darnholm and walk over the bracken hillside downstream.

To see Nelly Ayre Foss, as the sketch shows, you must walk from the sharp bend in the road west of Goathland village on a grass road that would take you further south to the Roman road above Wheeldale—this is generally known as Wade's Causeway. Wade was a Celtic or Saxon hero of such giant proportions that he threw the stones from somewhere above Sandsend to make a path for his wife to milk her cows, or was it the old lady herself who spilled them from her apron? To get home to Teesside, follow this narrow road west and then north from Goathland to cross the Esk at Egton Bridge—two miles further on you join the A171 for Guisborough.

Hole of Horcum

ONE of the most popular attractions in the North York Moors National Park is the Hole of Horcum, about seven miles north of Pickering on the A169. There is fairly ample parking space and a well patronised refreshment van. Many visitors of course simply sit on the sunny north-eastern slope and bask in the afternoon sunshine. The youngsters run up and down the steep grassy banks and scramble among the rocks very much as they do around Captain Cook's monument or on Roseberry Topping.

A half hour's walk to the east from the car park brings you to the edge of the escarpment above Newgate Foot. From this point you get an excellent view of the curiously isolated eminence known as Blakey Topping.

Legends assert that this huge mound was dug by a giant from the Hole of Horcum, but the truth is simple. The Hole has been excavated by the action of several springs wearing away the soft clay below the limestone beds. Blakey Topping, like Roseberry and Free-borough Hill, has been protected from the erosion of wind and rain by a cap of hard sandstone—Kellaway's Rock. Not far south of Blakey Topping are the Bride Stones, in a Naturalists' Trust Conservation area, but these curious natural phenomena are better approached from the south side, where there is a forestry car park.

The Hole of Horcum was formerly noted for its rare alpine and arctic plants—dwarf cornel and chickweed wintergreen are perhaps the best known, but here as elsewhere modern farming methods and over-zealous naturalists threaten these precious flowers with extinction. The county council did manage to check the enclosure of the Hole of Horcum by a timely purchase of much of the rough pasture, and the Moors National Park Committee opposed the plans of the Ministry of Agriculture to bring the Hole of Horcum and the moorlands neaby under the plough. It appears that, unlike the Roman citizens, we cannot have both bread and games in our National Park.

The Horcum car park, or better still the old coaching house on the elbow of Saltergate Hill, has always been a favourite starting point for trips to Newton Dale. This long narrow gorge is easily the most impressive of all the overflow channels carved out when the waters of Lake Eskdale burst over and through these high moorlands and poured down into the Vale of Pickering. The geological wonders of Newton gorge were readily observable by passengers on George Stephenson's railway which linked Grosmont and Pickering. This

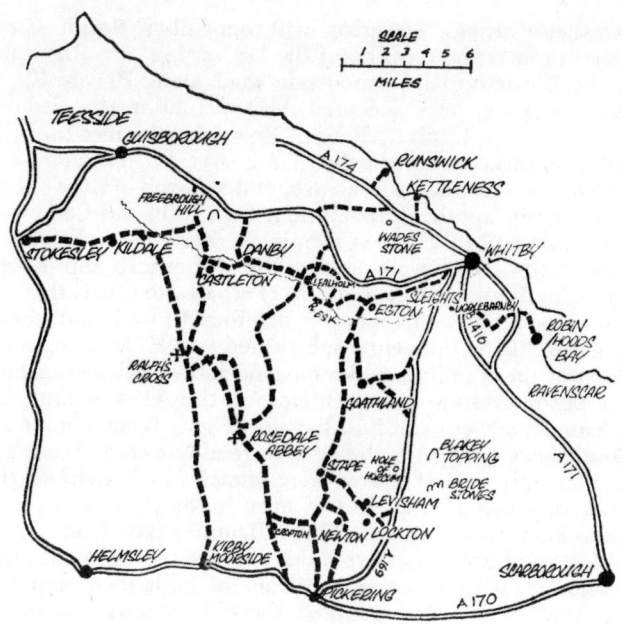

line fell victim to the Beeching axe, but has been re-opened by a preservation society.

For those discriminating travellers who seek to avoid the madding crowds at the Hole of Horcum car park on the A169, I would suggest an outing from one of three villages shown on the sketch map — Levisham, Lockton and Newton Rawcliffe. The narrow valley, with its quiet woods, which separates Lockton and Levisham, offers several tempting green lanes for a gentle afternoon or evening stroll and reasonable parking space on the broad greens in front of the village inns. Newton Dale itself can be approached from the east or west side as a well-used path links Newton and Lockton.

The moor roads in this area follow the lines of ancient ridgeways which may have been used a thousand years before the Romans came. The large standing stones that can be seen close to every roadside are guideposts set up by flint, salt or jet traders in Ancient Britain. The monks were also great traders in fish, fleece and iron. They re-marked the prehistoric ridgeways with crosses where the old stones had tumbled down or been taken away to repair local homesteads. Very frequently the new cross and the old pre-historic stones can still be found side by side.

This explains the existence of "Old Ralph" and "Young Ralph" on Castleton Rigg. Motorists will remember Ralph Cross very readily; it marks the meeting of the Westerdale and Rosedale roads with the Castleton Kirkbymoorside road along Blakey Rigg. Most of us, I imagine, have accepted the explanation that Ralph Cross commemorates a former Abbot of Rosedale who met the Abbess of Baysdale at this point where their lands shared a common boundary. But if you are one of those who pronounce Ralph to rhyme with waif, you will accept another explanation. Raif is the old Celtic word for rock or stone; Raif Cross is simply the cross near the stone. The syllable "raif" could well account for Ravenscar and Ravenscrag (above Clay Bank and Broughton). Perhaps, too, it is the origin of Robin Hood's Bay—this name is not found in any old charters or documents. "B" is frequently substituted for "V" as dialects change.

Many of the standing stones have no individual names but there is a rather interesting monolith close to the A174 behind the Outdoor Education Cetnre at East Barnby. This is Wade's Stone and it is obviously associated with the Roman road known as Wade's Causeway. It is only one of many huge stones which marked the pre-Roman ridgeway to the former busy harbour at Kettleness. The Romans knew this as Dunum Sinus—Dunsley Bay. Dun is the Celtic word for a hill and a high rounded hill used to dominate the little bay below Kettleness where the Romans built their signal station at Goldsborough. They adapted the old ridgeway in building a military road from the garrison town of Malton to the harbour and port at "Dunum Sinus". But the high hill was mutilated and brought low by the extensive excavations of the alum miners. The village and harbour disappeared beneath a great landslip one stormy December night in 1829. "The terrified inhabitants knew not which way to run: the sinking cliff pressed on them from behind, the yawning deep threatened them before." Fortunately they were rescued by an alum ship, the Henry, lying offshore.

If you venture along the rough road between Egton and Stape you will see quite a number of these marker stones. There is a pair of very tall columns with peep-holes bored at a height of a man's eye at the junction of the Stape and Goathland ridgeways. I have sketched in the Stape-Egton road because it is now possible to avoid a long detour via Pickering to cross Newton Dale. The Forestry Commission has built a road through Raindale Plantations from Levisham's former railway station to the Stape road. There is a charge of 10p.

Pickering Forest

THE fallow deer, the roe deer and the rare red deer are becoming so thick on the ground in our North Yorkshire forests that hunters are having to track them down. In a rapidly changing world it is pleasant to see the clock put back nearly 1,000 years. William the Conqueror "loved the tall deer as if he were their father". He and his successors cleared vast tracts of land to leave them open for the Royal deer. The Royal Forest of Pickering ranked only slightly lower than the New Forest, which lay so much closer to the king's capital city of Winchester.

Poaching of deer has become a serious problem in the Lake District forests but it is unlikely that the foresters will revive the penalties imposed by William (the Bastard, the English called him). Offenders were lucky to escape with blinding and the loss of the right hand. All dogs within the boundaries of the Royal parks and forests had one paw cut off: except, of course, the king's deerhounds.

Today, the Pickering Forest extends a welcome to visitors. It is the largest forest tract on upland moor in England and I, for one, find the varied beauties of its scenery far more pleasing and refreshing than the Pennine and Cheviot afforestations. There are wide parking places overlooking the sylvan valleys of Langdale, Troutsdale, Harwood Dale, Forge Valley, Staindale and half a dozen other tributaries of the River Derwent. The forestry headquarters is situated at the side of the A171 on the Eastgate, the main road leading out of Pickering. Here you may like to take advantage of the display of maps and booklets supplied by the Commission.

The forest trails which have been set up for walkers and the car routes have proved tremendously popular. The principal inform-ation centre is at Low Dalby and there are special booklets on sale dealing with five forest trails—Sneverdale, Wykeham, Silpho, Newton Dale and Falling Foss. You may also purchase a large-scale coloured map of these forestry attractions. I had rather a curious experience when I first used the forestry map. I took a quick glance and followed the line from Thornton Dale to Ellerburn hoping to travel northwards and reach Low Dalby. But I found the road deeply pot-holed and waterlogged: when I came to a locked gate I took another look at the map and found that I had mistaken the blue line of the Ellerburn Stream for the blue-green line of a forestry trail. As the lawyers say, "Caveat Emptor"—let him who buys

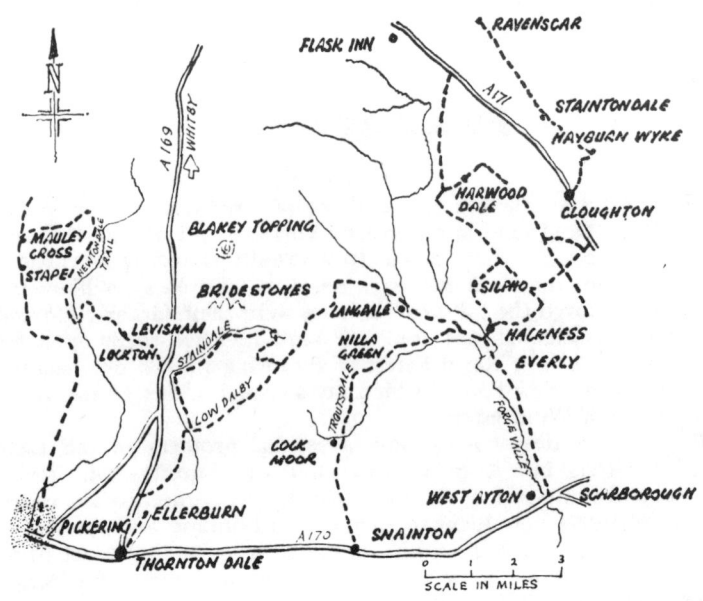

beware! Don't make my mistake — the line of the stream on a forestry map is thin and wavy: the roads thicker and straighter.

However, the experience was not without its reward. Ellerburn is a delightful village with parking behind the streamside tea gardens. The burn itself is a fast-flowing narrow trout stream which once drove the great wheels of two paper mills as well as the corn mills downstream at Thornton Dale. But times have changed and the settling pool of the paper mills is now a trout hatchery.

For the present the county council maintains the road as far as the Low Paper Mill. Beyond this point the forestry people built the road in the 1920s but once planting was finished the road had served its purpose and the foresters now use and maintain a good tarmac road which leaves the Thornton Dale — Whitby road about two miles north of Thornton. There is a coin box at the start of this route which gives access to the Bride Stones and the nature reserve from a pull-in point at the east end of Staindale.

One of the most popular routes starts from Snainton and runs up to Cock Moor Hall. A fine stretch of open, grass-covered moorland affords picnic space and extensive views over Troutsdale. There are good footpaths along the escarpment and they are deservedly popular with ramblers. The road along Troutsdale to Hilla Green and back to the A170 by Everley and Forge Valley is a grand run which will be at its best when the trees begin to take on their autumn colour. If you are wanting to get back to Teesside you can turn northwards through this delightful road winding its way among the tall trees of the Hackness parklands. From Silpho above Hackness the road takes a course with splendid vistas of tall trees and purple heather to join the A171 just south of that well-known landmark — the Flask Inn.

I have not made a habit of suggesting trips to the seaside — the routes are obvious and the beaches overcrowded. But I must mention one or two of the rocky "Wykes" which lie within easy reach of this eastern forestry area. There is a narrow gated lane leading off the Cloughton-Ravenscar road which crosses the old railway line and ends up at a very small gravelled parking area overlooking Cloughton Wyke. Here it joins the coastguards way, marked as the Roger Trod on the Ordnance Survey map. There are now few signs of any paved path, but the long-distance route now called the Cleveland Way is signposted along the cliff edge and it provides a most exhilarating experience as the waves make their music on the great rocks hundreds of feet below the rugged cliffs which gave the walk its name — Cleveland is of course the old Viking name for this land of cliffs. Further north is Hayburn Wyke. There is a private car park in front of the hotel at a modest charge. The tiny rock-strewn cove lies almost half a mile below and the path is narrow and rough but you should certainly find the journey well worth your while.

Kilburn's White Horse

ON a fine Sunday over 200 cars pull into the car park at Sutton Bank every hour. Travellers will now find a splendid new National Park Information Centre available here. No country lover should fail to take full advantage of the facilities offered to learn more about the area which the large map boards and the pamphlets illustrate so clearly. I particularly liked the geological model showing how the last Ice Age created the curious mixture of rounded knolls and deep lakes which are a feature of the Hambleton escarpment. The flood waters of the melting ice brought down the rich, black soil which makes the gardens of the villages on the western slopes so colourful. A mobile tea wagon close to the Information Centre provides light refreshment, but for the hungrier travellers there is the Hambleton Hotel close by. Here, above a roaring log fire, a certificate of Warm Welcome is proudly displayed. A wide choice of meals is offered up till ten o'clock in the evening. The choice runs from plain rolls and

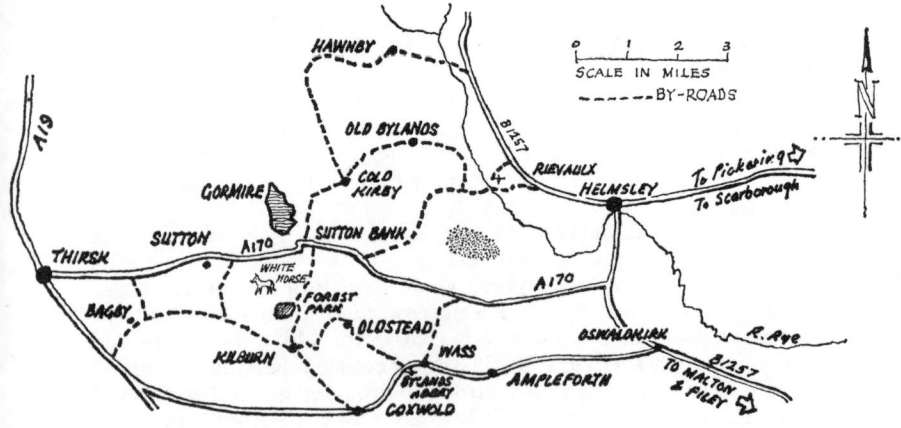

cheese to elaborate four course dinners.

The majority of motorists on the A170 are dashing straight on to Scarborough or Filey, and if they stop they merely take a brief look at the fine view from the escarpment edge. But there are many visitors whose stay is much longer. Gormire, with its Nature Trail, attracts not a few, but more go in the opposite direction towards the white cliffs of Roulston Scar.

There is a good path running between the cliff edge and the glider station. Half an hour's walk along this track brings you to Kilburn's famous White Horse, first carved out of the green turf in 1857. Just below the Horse is a spacious Forestry car park which I find preferable to the more crowded site on the top of Sutton Bank. The Forestry park lies close to the narrow road winding steeply uphill from Kilburn to the glider station and the A170 at the Hambleton Hotel.

The labour for Kilburn's White Horse was paid for in barrels of beer: the idea was the local schoolmaster's, but whether he was inspired by the Relief of Lucknow or by the gallant charge of the local lord of the Manor, Captain Wombwell, at Balaclava I cannot say. The White Horse tradition is of very ancient origin — possibly going back to the days when Boadicea's immediate forefathers with their horses and chariots drove out the more primitive peoples who sought refuge amongst their dykes and camps in these uplands. The Welsh Dragon emblem is simply a glorified version of the snorting, fiery war steed. Some local legends of a white horse are connected with the White Mare's Crag just to the north of Sutton Bank, rather than with Kilburn.

One story tells of an abbot of Rievaulx, far fonder of the chase than the chapel, who was the proud owner of a white Arab mare, famed for its beauty and its speed. Nearby lived a noble knight, Harry de Scriven, whose black Barbary stallion was equally famous. Harry was jealous of the abbot and ever ready to play a trick on his rival. One night when Harry found the abbot "winkin and blinkin in the hostelry on Hambleton Heath" he tried to lure him away on the pretence that a dying farmer needed to be shriven. They exchanged horses and drove off through the darkness. Sir Harry could not manage the wild Arab and the abbot lured him to the edge of the cliff and over he went. The abbot on the black horse remained suspended in air: the old rhyme ends —

Two horns on the head of the abbot were growing.
His feet cloven hoofed in the stirrups were showing,
"If you must play a trick
Try it not on Old Nick
I'll see you below when I visit the sick."

A prominent landmark between Kilburn and Sutton Bank is Hood Hill, on top of which was the Hood stone marked by the devil's foot print. This rock was reputed to weigh 30 tons, and to have been about the size of a large domestic garage. Even in this scientific age legends still accumulate about the stone. Two "reliable sources" who live close below the stone have assured me that a Meteor Jet crashed into the stone and split it asunder, but no traces of the plan could be found, nor can I get any confirmation of a recent crash from the local police. Does the devil still look after his own?

I mention the bracing walk above Roulston Scar. If you wish to complete a circular tour between the two car parks there is a good bridle road from the Kilburn Forestry park below the Scar which comes out at the elbow of the last steep bend on Sutton Bank. If you have the official Ordnance Survey Map of the National Park you will also see a bridle road marked through the farm of Hood Grange and continuing north-westwards to Sutton village. This road has recently been ploughed up in two fields adjoining the farm and the way is not visible on the ground. The track is a very ancient route — the foundations of a metalled road were unearthed some eight feet below the present level of the ground: local opinion readily accepted the idea that this was a Roman road, but the professional archaeologist will look for a rather later dating.

Hood Grange was a moated site in the troubled times of Stephen and Matilda when "God and his Saints slept"; the barons pillaged and looted without restraint and erected many "Adulterine" castles without royal licence. Roger de Mowbray had erected one such unlicensed castle at Hood, but when he saw the error of his ways he gave the site to a holy hermit who began to cultivate a patch of ground in this sheltered spot. Later other priests settled here and a group of Cistercians came from Furness Abbey. Later they moved a few miles further east and founded Byland, to which abbey the great warrior Roger de Mowbray himself retired when weary of war.

It is a wise and pleasant thing to avoid the West Yorkshire traffic both along the "High Street", the A170, from Thirsk to Scarborough or the very popular route through Coxwold, Ampleforth and Oswaldkirk which joins the B1257 to continue to Malton and Filey. The narrow winding lanes through Kilburn, Oldstead and Wass with their high hedges and colourful grass verges are much more attractive for leisurely sightseeing. You can rejoin the A170 from Oldstead or Kilburn by passable but steep roads which converge on the Hambleton Hotel. A mile east of this inn a secondary road goes through Scawton and Rievaulx to the B1257 linking Helmsley and Stokesley. Kilburn is the home of the wooden mouse and the famous wood-carving establishment of the Thompsons lies close to the imposing Foresters' Arms with its Olde English Tudor timber frame. By contrast, the Abbey Inn close to Byland Abbey, a mile or so further on, does not seem to have changed in 40 years.

From Wass there is a good by-road straight up the hillside to the A170. There is a complicated road junction but turn left for the Scawton and Rievaulx return route; alternatively, turn right and swing in a great arc round Duncombe Park to return to Teesside via Helmsley. If you do have time to linger in Coxwold there are several spots of "special interest". The sponsors of the Laurence Sterne Museum at Shandy Hill will appreciate your support. The church on its flower bedecked eminence is a most imposing site, whilst not far to the south is the seat of the Wombwells, Newburgh Priory, where the bones of Oliver Cromwell lie buried. By some curious anomaly of history, while Cromwell is alleged to have cut down all the royal oaks on the estate, the Wombwells certainly made up the loss by importing plants and seed from Australia and California to provide the magnificent woods on the Cam banks above Wass.

Ryedale

FEW districts offer wider prospects than the old Wapentake of Ryedale—the western half of the colourful Vale of Pickering. Here there are tidy, bright villages built in the clean, white limestone so abundantly available on the low hills to north and south of the vale. The gardens are a refreshing treat for the eye—a great change from the massed roses which seem to thrive so well on Teesside's heavy clay. I was particularly struck with the glorious pinks of massed Godetia, which an old gardener assured me would provide flowers for the hall table until November.

The villagers take a just pride in the appearance of their home-steads and their village greens: they are encouraged by various organisations such as the Council for the Protection of Rural England and the Yorkshire Rural Community Council. This latter body organises an annual "best-kept village" competition. It is not surprising that leading awards have been won by villages in this area.

This is the Land of the Seven Rivers in more senses than one: not only does the River Seven flow into the vale from the watershed along which the Lyke Wake walkers tread high above the head of Rosedale, but the Rye, the Riccal and the Dove join with the Hodge Beck and the Ellerburn to link with the main stream of the Derwent from Forge Valley. The Derwent is one of Nature's freaks. It flows away from the sea towards York, 50 miles inland from its source. Like the Leven, which formerly flowed into the sea near Whitby, the Derwent's mouth was dammed up by the Cheviot and the Scandin-avian glaciers and the river dug a broad new channel to the west when the ice began to melt. If you want to make the most of the seven rivers you should spend an hour or two watching the deep pools which can be seen not far from the road verges at many points—Nunnington Bridge is my favourite spot.

The fat, lazy trout of Ryedale are almost a legend although not all are quite the equal of the Jubilee Trout on display in a glass case in the butcher's shop overlooking the dark pool below Helmsley Bridge. I cannot accurately quote his (or her?) vital statistics but two feet long and seven inches from dorsal fin down to whatever a trout uses for a navel seems to be about right. You may see a heron winging a deceptively lazy way above these waters; the greedy bird often spears a fish apparently only for practice, for anglers tell me they find dead fish holed by a heron's beak on the river banks.

For centuries this rich farmland has ensured a prosperity which has left its evidence in the stately homes of the gentry, the successors

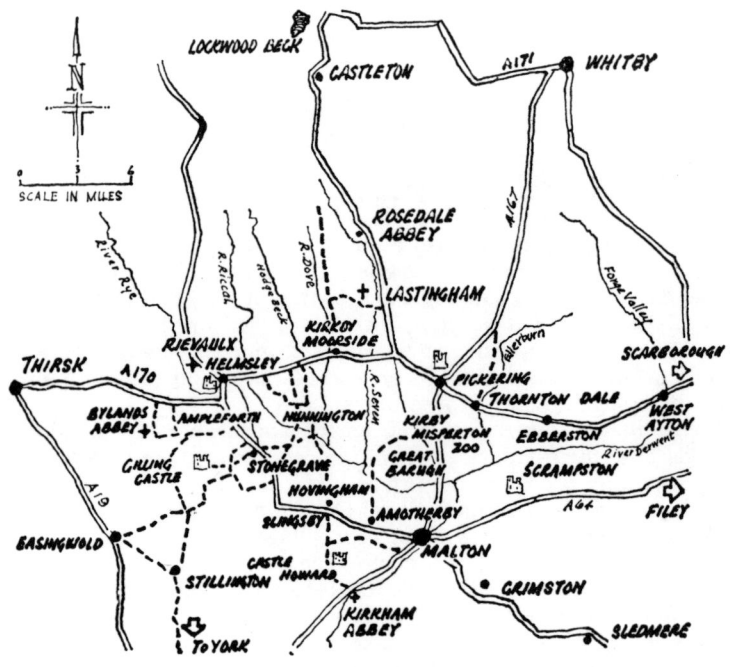

of the abbots who built their houses to the greater glory of God in an earlier age. Almost every village can boast an imposing hall, built in the best traditions of the time. There is Nunnington Hall, now a National Trust property open to the public on Wednesdays. Castle Howard with its lake, parkland, furniture, tapestries and best of all its collection of costumes is perhaps the most well known of all our Yorkshire country houses and is open daily with good refreshment facilities and ample parking space. My own favourite is Gilling Castle—now a preparatory school for Ampleforth College. Not all this building is open to the public gaze, but the Great Hall can usually be seen in the late morning and mid afternoon on weekdays, although the best time to visit is during school holidays.

What a picture it makes! Especially for those with an interest in heraldry. The great screen round the fireplace is emblazoned with dozens of coats of arms in full heraldic colour. The frieze below the panelled ceiling is decorated with trees, each hung with heraldic shields to represent local villages. The magnificent bay windows are also aglow with coloured glass—of several different ages and types. All this glorious history might well have decorated some Hollywood boudoir but for a curious twist of fate. Randolph Hearst, the

34

American millionaire film impresario and founder of the Hearst Press, bought the panelling, the glass and the great screen, but the war prevented their being shipped from London to the States. They were discovered, dirty but comparatively undamaged, after the war and returned to their original home—forever, let us hope! The cricket ground, first laid out by the great Ranjitsinghi, lies to the east of the school. The superb gardens can be seen in the shelter of the valley which formed the moat of the mediaeval castle, on the north-west.

In Ryedale the narrow lanes run from village to village and the main roads reel to right and left, as G.K. Chesterton so aptly described them—as if designed by drunken men. Although main roads run through Hovingham from Helmsley to York, and through Nunnington from Kirkbymoorside—they are very narrow and tortuous in places. They cannot easily be made much wider, nor can the bends be avoided except by cutting down magnificent avenues of centuries old elms and sycamores which provided shade for the coach horses and pack ponies of bygone years. The same difficulty arises with the narrow, arched bridges which cross the seven rivers. The crossing points had to be carefully selected where the rivers narrowed and the banks were firm. Frequently older roads had to leave their earlier line of march and diverge in a wide loop to utilise new bridges.

For many motorists the A170 and the A64 are merely short cuts to the sea at Scarborough, Filey and Bridlington or even to Kirby Misperton Zoo in Flamingo Park, but to lovers of old England it is well worth seeing the quieter ways between these main roads. There is scarcely a village without some ancient relic.

Many of the churches hereabouts, like St. Gregory's Minster at Kirkdale, contain warm brown sandstone worked into later limestone fabric of Norman and Gothic churches. Many of these sandstones show decoration far superior to anything brought over or achieved by the Norman conquerors of our Saxon predecessors. Stonegrave has a magnificent carved Saxon cross and a gravestone marked with a pair of shears—obviously the tomb of some great but unknown Saxon princess. Appleton-le-Street has a Saxon three-storied tower not unlike Teesside's Billingham Church of St. Cuthbert. It also has a similar shafted window in the bell tower.

Both these Ryedale churches, and many others in the area, have tiny carved figures, grotesque perhaps, but created with a skill and art far beyond that of any Norman masons. There is a tradition that St. Wilfrid of Ripon founded a school of stonemasons who developed a high degree of competence and a distinctly artistic style: this may account for the use of sandstone rather than the local limestone. A final note! Even the grass seems greener in this blessed spot and it is no surprise to notice Malton and Sledmere on the sketch map—Sledmere has pastured many young thoroughbreds who once made the virtues of the English race-horse famed all over the sporting world.

Upleatham Church, near Redcar.

Part Two:

Some
Detailed Routes

Helmsley Market Cross (John Parker)

Teesside - Wilton - Upleatham - Liverton-
Sandsend - Ugthorpe - Staithes - Teesside

WAS it the Prime Minister of Mirth who used to sing "I stopped, and I looked and I listened"? Perhaps with the passing of so many branch lines and the rustic level crossings, this practice has become outmoded. Nevertheless if you get off the main roads, it is still possible and profitable to stop, to look and listen. Any map can show you where to go, from town to town or village to village. When to stop is a matter for long search and experiment, particularly if you want the solace of solitary places, rather than the boisterous clamour of crowded beaches.

This run finds us winding a slow, tortuous way among the wooded valleys which stretch from the high moors to the coast. Stop and investigate: take a long look at the wide variety of gay flowers and above all listen to the sounds. The blackcap, an occasional wren or warbler and a few other sylvan songsters may be heard. The plaint of the peewit and the haunting cry of the curlew on the open heaths above Moorsholm blend with the cooing of the cushat in the deep ravines below. The distant wind in the high treetops above a sheltered valley, the murmur of hidden waters in a cool wood on a hot summer's day, the hum of myriads of unseen insects in the undergrowth along our woodland paths, all these are a constant delight and a stimulant to town-jaded nerves.

This tour starts off along the Parkway, the new A174. About half a mile beyond the wide Eston roundabout take the diversion to Wilton village and climb the winding lane. At the bend near the top of the hill there is a convenient entry for a walk into the woods where there is an attractive lily pond and a variety of paths both broad and narrow which offer opportunity for pleasant rambles of a length to suit all ages and strengths. If you continue along the lane from the top of the hill you strike the A173 at the east end of Guisborough and turn left towards Skelton. Follow the A173 for a mile and a half. Then turn left over the bridge to Upleatham (B1268). If you have not visited the tiny chapel on the right of the road just beyond this village, take this opportunity. Below the chapel, there is a little stretch of woodland with Skelton Castle on the far side of the valley.

The road through Upleatham turns south at the next junction to reach Skelton where the A173 is rejoined and followed to the east end of the village. Fork right to Lingdale at the cemetery to reach the A171, the moor road, at Lockwood Beck reservoir. You leave the A171 less than half a mile farther on. A narrow lane winds left to Moorsholm, from which village there are three fairly well used

Cowbar, near Staithes (Keith Robson)

entrances to Kilton woods on the west and south. Turn to the right at the end of the village and drop down to the delightful little valley at Liverton Mill. At the hairpin bend there is a broad drive on the left leading into the woods, with quite an impressive waterfall about half a mile downstream. Much further downstream, too far perhaps for a visit on this occasion, is Kilton Castle, where formerly the gay banner of the Three Green Popinjays fluttered high on the tall crags above the stream.

Climbing up beyond the mill you reach Liverton village itself at the B1366. The little church has some quaint carvings which must be almost a thousand years old. At the bend beyond Liverton take the right fork and as you pass a large farm on your right keep a look out for a seat in the hedge side on your left. At that point you may enter the woods, either on your left or across the field on your right. Continue downhill and you reach Loftus and the coast road to Whitby (A174). Follow this road to Lythe and drop down the steep bank to Sandsend if you wish to spend a few hours strolling round Mulgrave woods.

The woods around the modern Mulgrave Castle, home of the Marquis of Normanby, are open to visitors on Wednesdays,

Saturdays and Sundays. They are perhaps at their best when the rhododendrons bloom, but their well-maintained paths and carefully tended trees make them attractive at any season of the year.

The older medieval castle stands on a narrow ridge between Sandsend Beck and East Beck. It has interesting connections with Magna Carta and Women's Lib. King John had given the hand of Isabella de Turnham of Mulgrave Castle to his strongarm man, Peter de Mauley, who had blinded and murdered Prince Arthur, the rightful heir to Richard Coeur de Lion. The Northern Barons, calling themselves the Army of God, protested strongly and eventually forced John to grant the Great Charter. Two clauses of the Charter declared that the King could not marry an heiress against her wish and those of her family. Any heiress once married to a man of the King's choice could choose a second husband if she became a widow.

Returning from Sandsend, come back up to Lythe and turn left in the middle of this little village. A narrow tree-lined road winds up and down with several picturesque dells inviting a picnic. Ugthorpe is the next village, with its strong traditions of loyalty to the Old Faith, tales of priests' hidey-holes and underground passages. Ugthorpe House, in seventeenth century style, was let for one shilling per annum by the Merry Monarch, Charles II, to two ladies. As far as I know, the citation of services rendered for this award was as vague and inconclusive as that of the Beatles. However, "honi soit ..."

Fork left to the moor road, A171, and follow this to Scaling Dam. Turn right at the garage to see the best of all these little roads through the ravines. This is the popular and aptly named Ridge Lane. In places scarcely wide enough to take even one large car, the ridge runs between Scaling and Roxby Becks to Staithes. The woods on both sides are at their best in primrose time, but the paths are steep and slippery, especially in damp weather. At Staithes, turn left along the A174 and through the Cleveland mining villages back to Teesside.

Teesside - Commondale - Fryupdale - Egton - Rosedale - Westerdale - Teesside

LEAVE Teesside by the A172 and turn left for Ayton at the B1292 junction. Turn right again at Guisborough Road and in Ayton cross straight over the bridge and make for Kildale. Follow the signposts to Commondale and Castleton and when you reach the top of the hill in Castleton village take the road down towards Danby. Take the second turn to the right signposted Ainthorpe and Fryup. Once again take the second turn left to climb steeply up to the open moor just beyond the Fox and Hounds in Ainthorpe village.

As the road swings to the left at the top of the hill gaze for a moment at what could claim to be the most isolated and windswept tennis court in England. As the road drops into Fryupdale it runs between high walls and steep grassy banks. Here there are wandering sheep who sensibly prefer the lush grass of the lane to the coarse heather of the high moorland. After a mile along this lane you come to Danby Castle, seen on the left. Exiled Scots may find some sentimental pride in remembering that this was once Bruce territory, but very little remains for the military architect to study.

Your route turns south along Little Fryupdale and then swings east over Fairy Cross plain into Great Fryup. As you drop steeply down into a wood you turn sharp left and go northwards down Great Fryupdale. Fork right at the T-junction for Lealholm about two and a half miles from this wood.

As you climb up from the bridge over Great Fryup Beck you ignore two right turns and swing to the left, passing through an open farmyard where a gaggle of geese or a flush of mallard may impede your progress. At the next T-bend beyond this farmyard turn down left to Lealholm. Go straight through the village and take the second right turn at the top of the hill for Whitby. You are now in a delightful lane which winds down a steep hairpin at Stonegate Mill. Two miles beyond the mill you strike the A171 but immediately leave it by the right turn to Egton.

Drop steeply down through Egton; ignore the first turn to the right near the railway bridge but turn right to cross the river by the narrow bridge. As you come out from the trees near the bridge, two tall Scots pines tower high above, framing the banks above Arncliffe Gorge, and sheltering the attractive Horseshoe Inn on your right. The tea garden by the riverside satisfies more than one appetite.

Ignore the left turn for Goathland and Stape and go straight ahead. The narrow sunken lane climbs up to the open moor through the tiny hamlet of Delves. On the moor top the road runs across wild moorland, unfenced for about nine miles. You may fail to

Danby Castle (Elizabeth Gray)

notice Hamer House, now almost levelled to the ground. Not so many years ago it offered refreshment to drovers and the miners who worked outcrops of coal in this area. Now only the Lyke Wake walkers huddle behind its heaps of stone as they take their soup or cocoa on the last stages of their trek to Ravenscar.

Soon after crossing a lonely gill in the heart of the moor you must take a right fork and drop down into Rosedale. Turn right below the inn for Castleton and then take the first fork up to the right a mile beyond the village. This road joins the Castleton - Hutton-le-Hole road after a further five miles. Turn right and take the left fork through Westerdale. This road has been much improved and cattle grids have replaced several gates. This brings you back into Kildale. Return to Teesside by your outward route.

Middlesbrough-Seamer-Hutton Rudby-Carlton - Chop Gate - Battersby - Guisborough - Middlesbrough

FROM Middlesbrough or Thornaby proceed to the roundabout at the beginning of the Parkway, and take the signposted road to Maltby. Just opposite the "Pathfinders" take the right turn to Hilton. When you reach the south end of this village take the left turn to Seamer at the T-junction. Go right through Seamer, avoiding the left turn to Ayton, and just beyond the village swing to the left to Stokesley, unless you are fond of gated field roads.

If this is so, take the right fork at this bend in the Stokesley road. The surface is reasonable and it reaches the Stokesley - Hutton Rudby road near Skutterskelfe Hall. However, if you don't risk this field you continue up Seamer Hill beyond the village and continue in the direction of Stokesley until you strike the T-junction at the bungalows of Tame Bridge. Turn right here and just beyond the high walls of Skutterskelfe Park you see the field road from Seamer coming up on your right. Half a mile down the bank turn left and drop down to Hutton Rudby church. You climb the steep hill from the church, pass the village green and take the first sharp turn left to Sexhow just near the school. There is a charming spot for a picnic or a leg-stetcher as you cross a ford close to the Leven, but, like many another quiet corner, it is becoming increasingly popular.

This lane, with other glimpses of the Leven valley and Skutterskelfe Park on the left, crosses the A174 to reach Carlton. Turn right and go up to the hills through Carlton village. At the top of the hill there is a fine open stretch of grassland but please do not add to the collection (or is it dispersal?) of tins and bottles already disfiguring the car park. The views here are good. Occasionally there are motor cycle scrambles. Youngsters can climb about the rocks and shale heaps and gazing at the gliders can have a soothing effect on the jaded town nerves of their elders.

From Carlton Bank top continue down into Raisdale and turn left at Chop Gate to the little car park at the top of Clay Bank. If you pause here you can send the more vigorous of your party to emulate the Cleveland mountaineers on the Wainstones or simply watch the perspiring Lyke Wake walkers as they come down from Hasty Bank and toil up to Round Howe. From the Hasty Bank car park take the winding road down to the east. Swing round in a wide half circle into Ingleby village and continue on to Old Battersby. This is a really colourful village with long, old fashioned vegetable and flower gardens in front of each cottage.

Beyond Battersby take the right fork to Kildale. At the head of the dale take the road down to the right towards Westerdale. As you begin to drop down into the rather gloomy, narrow valley of Baysdale Beck turn sharp left at a bend in the road and follow the signpost to Commondale and Castleton. The road forks after about two miles and you turn sharp left across the open moor to reach Commondale. Turn right at the T-junction in the middle of the village. At the top of the hill you turn left, joining the main stream of traffic back to Teesside via Lockwood Beck and Guisborough.

Teesside-Kirklevington-Appleton Wiske-Scarth Nick - Upsall - Rievaulx - Teesside

TAKE the old A19 from Yarm to Kirklevington. Turn right along Forest Lane, past the ancient Saxon church on to the bright, fashionable gardens of the commuters and the cosier "old English" enclosures round the stone cottages. Note on the right the prominent, newly-restored sundial that marks a former inn; we wondered if an over-indulgent host delayed calling time until he saw the first shadow cast by the rising sun! At the end of Forest Lane turn left and proceed to Appleton Wiske.

Here, turn sharp left and follow the signposted lanes to West Rounton and then in a long detour back to East Rounton — the Rountons ancient and modern. The former old world cottages, the latter dignified Edwardian brick with generous overhanging roofs and well-barbered lawns. Go to the left as you climb the hill into East Rounton and look out for the charming lych-gate and porch on the left. Half a mile north of the village turn right and take the next T-bend to the right to reach Trenholme on the A19. You turn south for two miles and leave the A19 by a narrow lane opposite the ICI pumps.

You are making for the A172 to Swainby which you strike at Ingleby Arncliffe after passing straight through the newer houses at Ingleby Cross. The curious brown stone edifice at the first village is a bit of Victorian Gothic. Contrast it with Hutton Rudby's water tower in Elizabethan concrete. You will have noticed this when you were bowling along from Trenholme. From Ingleby Arncliffe you turn left along the A172 and take a right turn at the first crossroads. This narrow lane leads up to Scarth Nick and Osmotherley — watch out for the concealed fork as you reach a patch of woodland. At the Sheep Wash car parks the Cod Beck is a grand playground for the youngsters but they will not catch sight even of the tiniest tiddler as strangely enough there are no fish in this inaptly-named stream.

Continue due south through Osmotherley and Thimbleby. Strike the A19 once again and turn left for about five miles. Note on your left the stoutly-built Saxon tower of Leake Church, sole surviving relic of a handsome village, once a victim of the marauding Scots. A mile beyond the church, look carefully for the turn-off to Knayton on the left. Go due east through the village and take the first turn right, climbing gently to Upsall. Note the well-kept hedges in the lanes hereabouts. In the centre of Upsall turn left to Kirby Knowle. Note the imposing hall perched high up on the left of the road. This is the "new" building, dating back to the seventeenth century; the old castle at Upsall lies below the main part of the village.

In Kirby Knowle take the fork to the right, just opposite the imposing church, signposted Felixkirk. In less than half a mile take the narrow road on your left to Boltby. At the end of this charming village, with its long, colourful gardens, climb over the ridge and drop down past the waterworks and Hesketh Hall before beginning the tortuous ascent to Sneck Yat on the Hambleton Drove Road. Here you turn right and proceed for about two miles; then take the left turn to Old Byland and Rievaulx.

As I mentioned earlier, this narrow lane by-passes the first village and turns along the high wooded banks of Ryedale where you get a fine view of this, surely the loveliest of our dales. Avoid the first turn left down to Tylas Farm—the surface is none too good although you can get to Rievaulx this way. You find yourself dropping steadily down to the graceful bridge near Ashberry Farm, where you cross the stream. Re-cross it again by the bridge half a mile farther on and do, please, stop and look back at the wonderful riverside garden near the high arch of the bridge. From Rievaulx go straight up to the A172 and so back to Teesside.

Old Byland church (Alec Wright)

46

Stokesley-Mount Grace Priory-Cowesby-Kilburn-Byland Abbey-Rievaulx Abbey-Bilsdale - Stokesley

THE first reaction of visitors to Rievaulx, Mount Grace or Byland is almost invariably: "What an eye those old boys had for scenery! They certainly picked their spots." This, of course, is less than a half truth. The fact is that when the monks first set up their cells these places were desolate. As the old chronicler says of Rievaulx: it was set in a place "most desolate and solitary, overgrown with dense thorns and inhabited only by the wildest of beasts". This description could have applied to most of the North Riding for many years after the Conquest, when William laid waste the north and the Domesday Book records "Hoc est vasta", this is waste, in village after village.

Today the tree-screened banks of the Rye and its flower-starred meadows form a fitting frame for the mellowed stone arches of the abbey church. St. Ailred and his fellow workers tamed the wilderness and made this desolate and solitary spot one of the most peaceful and attractive corners in Yorkshire. The same can be said of other abbey sites locally. Until two wars took toll of the magnificent woods on Arncliffe, Mount Grace had an equally lovely setting. Thanks largely to the chatelaine of the Priory, Miss Cooper Abbs, the abbey church still retains a sheltering screen though on a much smaller scale than Rievaulx. Byland, of course, is sheltered on the north by a first rate stretch of woodland planted more than a century ago by the Wombwell family, whose coat of arms may be seen on many of the well-designed cottages in this area; more particularly the superbly-sited cottage near Rievaulx bridge.

The route recommended here, with its balanced mixture of main road and country lane, will take the motorist through these monastic domains. Devout donors left these lands to the church "for the salvation of their own souls and the greater glory of God" as many a charter and deed relates. Thus it is in more than one sense that this corner of the county may claim to be God's own country. When you set out for Mount Grace use the A172 via Ingleby Arncliffe. The afternoon sun on the crags and quarries of Carlton Bank and Cringle Moor brings out their full colour and fascinating shapes.

A profitable and restful hour may be spent on Mount Grace. The abbey is almost the only one of its kind in a reasonable state of preservation. A few learned brothers lived there, each in his private study with bedroom, herb garden and running water. The water came from a delightful spring on the northeast corner of the quadrangle which has only recently been uncovered.

From Mount Grace follow the Thirsk road A19 for about five miles

Thatched cottage at Rievaulx (Bernard Fearnley)

and turn off to the left at a signpost "To Silton". This narrow lane is lined with ash and oak. It will give you a chance to decide the old riddle as to which comes first, or of course you may wish to forecast the summer's weather:

"Ash before Oak, in for a soak!
Oak before Ash, beware of a splash."

Take the first turn right along the road towards Kepwick and Helmsley. You can admire the topiary of the expertly clipped hedges on your right. Near Kepwick you should once again turn right. This is a feature of the trip. You approach village after village from below on the west side and then swing away in a half circle towards the next hamlet. Spare a few minutes to go into Cowesby, its curious grey-green church spire will probably have caught your attention as you approached the village. Cowesby has a local reputation of being the cosiest of all these villages. It is certainly a suntrap and the high hills which almost completely enclose it, protect if from all the harsh storms of winter and the northerly mists which torment this part of the world in springtime.

On again following the winding lane, sighting Boltby then turning right to Thirlby. Beyond this tiny hamlet tower the great limestone crags of Rawcliff and Whitestone Cliff. Farther on you will join the A170 just below the notorious Sutton Bank. Turn up towards the hills and just beyond the village take the right turn for Kilburn, passing the compact but dignified Osgodby Hall behind its stately garden walls on your left. As you drop into Kilburn the glorious panorama of the vales of York and Pickering will be unrolled before you. This is the view to show any foreign or colonial visitors. No country in the world can boast so colourful a patchwork of pasture and ploughland, park and wood, as this superb stretch between Black Hambleton and the green Howardian Hills.

Beyond Kilburn you have the choice of a shaded, twisting road known as the Ragged Way, to Byland and Wass via Oldstead, or the broader road through Coxwold. If you take this route you can see the old vicarage in which Laurence Sterne wrote his classic novel "Tristram Shandy". The magnificent octagonal tower of the church just opposite is worth seeing. Pause at Byland, even if it is only to wonder at the amazing mosaic pavements of the chapel, a work that testifies to the development and patience of medieval craftsmen. There was certainly no time and motion study to save labour costs in the twelfth century.

From Byland go straight up the hill beyond Wass and turn left along the A170, the Hambleton Street. Just beyond the eighth milestone from Thirsk, turn off along the narrow road to Scawton and Rievaulx. There is no need for me to repeat myself on the glories of Rievaulx, nor can any mere words describe the feeling of utter restfulness which even a short visit to this quiet valley can inspire. Along Bilsdale by the B1257, through Chop Gate and Great Broughton to Stokesley is the route home.

Teesside - Hutton Rudby - Scarth Nick - Osmotherley - Kepwick - Hawnby - Bilsdale - Teesside

HALF-HIDDEN among the hedgerow shrubs at Laskill, on the main road through Bilsdale, stands a modest white-washed building. It is the Friends' Meeting House: scarcely big enough to be described as a cottage, too substantial to be termed a hut. Contrast this humble religious edifice with the great pile of majestic ruins at Rievaulx, two or three miles farther down the valley. There is a moral to be drawn somewhere.

For Laskill, as the medieval carvings incorporated in the modern farmhouse bear witness, was the headquarters of the abbey's business. Here were collected the thousands of fleeces which were sold annually to the cloth merchants of Flanders and Tuscany. Here, too, was the site of the flourishing ironworks which helped the monks to pay the masons who built the tall choir church and the lordly lodgings of the Abbot of Rievaulx. The ostentatious wealth of the Cistercians led to their dissolution by the first Defender of the Faith and all that is left of these early ironmasters is the quiet beauty of Ryedale, a contrast and a relief to the dark satanic mills founded by the Quakers in the Ironmasters' District of Teesside.

You should leave Teesside by the A1044, the old road linking Guisborough and Richmond. Builders and local council have named it Low Lane, Yarm Road, and so on, but the most common and proper term is Ladgate Lane, for it was along this route that lead from the Swaledale and Teesdale mines was carried to roof the great Priory at Guisborough. Opposite the inn at High Leven you leave the A1044 and turn off to the left to Hilton. Stop at the church if you are interested in pre-Norman relics. There are a number of bits of Saxon masonry to be seen in the churchyard. Half a mile beyond the village turn off to the right and follow a narrow winding road almost to Middleton-on-Leven. Just as you near the village a sharp turn to the left finds your car going due south to Hutton Rudby, leaving Middleton on your right.

As you approach the top of a gentle rise you may spot the words Spyknave Hill on a farm gate to the left. This unusual name puzzled me considerably. Could it be the site of an ancient watch tower built by lords of the old motte and bailey castle just behind us at Middleton? About a mile beyond Spyknave Hill you meet the road from Stokesley coming in on your left, but you must keep straight ahead to the curious combination of "Hutton, Rudby, Enterpen! Here there be no honest men". This rhyme dates back to the old days of the Guilds, when the clothiers hereabouts had a bad reputation for over-stretching their lengths of cloth.

Unless you reach the bridge at church time you should find some parking space between Rudby and Hutton. The Leven is very attractive at this point, tumbling from one deep pool to another between high wooded banks. There is a good streamside footpath opposite the church for a pleasant stroll to stretch your legs, and the silent challenge of the trout to excite the children as they play about the banks. Continue straight through the village with a glance at the long shaded green on your right. There are "No Parking" signs at this point, so one must keep moving.

Take the first turn left beyond the village and run beneath the arch of the tall beeches and limes that surround the parklands of Linden Grove on the east side of this quiet lane. You strike Potto at the top of a gentle rise and turn right in the middle of the village. The next turn is to the left at the end of the high walled garden of Potto Hall. Go straight across the A172 and follow the narrow road up to Scarth Nick and the popular picnic spot of Sheep Wash. This is National Trust property and there is great freedom of movement but with the usual wise conventions, no camping, no fires. Some visitors have obviously been great admirers of the short moorland turf, but it is as foolish as it is unfair to take huge slices of this turf back to your town gardens. It will not thrive on the heavy clays of Teesside and to try it leaves an ugly scar on the face of this lovely countryside.

Go straight on and through Osmotherley village to Thimbleby, always gay in apple blossom time, for there is hardly a garden without its flowering trees or shrubs. Beyond Thimbleby you reach the A19 and follow it south for a couple of miles and then turn to the left along Leake Lane to Kepwick. The road winds steeply up through the woodland behind Kepwick Hall. At the top of the hill is a broad white gate. You cross the ancient drovers' road and continue eastwards, climbing gently for another half mile or so across the undulating open moor. This narrow, gated, white limestone track is not nearly so uncomfortable as it looks. There have been trunk roads in northern county boroughs far more discouraging to car-proud travellers.

As you begin to drop down from the open moor to the dark woods of Arden you reach the last of the gates. Here is the best viewpoint, over the wall on your left. In the depths of a narrow valley gleams the unruffled water of a tiny lake. The whole setting might have sprung straight from a travel poster advertising some Norwegian fjord. There are more delightful glimpses of woodland and parkland as you drop gently down towards Hawnby. Ignore the right turn to Helmsley just after you pass the village inn and continue straight ahead to a very steep drop with sharp bends and a narrow bridge but not much warning.

You climb up the shoulder of Easterside Hill and get splendid views of Ryedale and Bilsdale, the former green, grass-covered limestone country, the other fringed by the Blackamoor of the sandstone. Eventually you drop gently down in a wide half circle to cross Bilsdale's river Seph. A short climb and a swing to the left brings you to the Friends' Meeting House at Laskill and the junction with the B1257. Turn left for Stokesley and Teesside.

Teesside - Bilsdale - Hawnby - Sutton Bank - Slingsby - Kirby Mills - Teesside

IN early summer the north east suffers from persistent polar air streams, but they can be avoided by a judicious application of geographical principles. Now that comprehensive education is fashionable, every schoolchild should know about rain shadow areas and your offspring will be able to tell you that when the "roak" hides the cliffs at Boulby and Ravenscar, the vale of Pickering should be basking in sunshine, beneath the shelter of the high moorlands, so you will set off in search of the sun along the B1257 towards Helmsley. You climb up out of Bilsdale by the Newgate Bank; the "Old gate" ran farther to the east and crossed Roppa Banks to Carlton.

The view from Newgate Bank Top is deservedly considered one of the finest in Yorkshire. No doubt your offspring could give you another geography lesson at this point. Behind, to the east and north, lies the barren Blackamoor, growing little but heather and bracken on the tops, with indifferent pasture in the broad valleys. To the south and east the narrow valleys are thickly wooded and the broad uplands are covered with rich pastures and ploughlands on a limestone base. Between the limestone mass and the northern sandstone lie the curious isolated hills, the outliers—Hawnby, Easterside and Combe Hill.

From Newgate Bank go ahead to the first turn right which takes you back along the valley of the Rye towards Hawnby. This will give you a chance to admire the magnificent woods that extend from Helmsley for almost five miles upstream on the left bank of the river. As you approach Hawnby village you must turn very sharply left up the bank to Murton Heights. You are now on the Peak Scar road that links Hawnby and Sutton Bank Top. A couple of hundred yards from the top of Murton Bank you may see a little hand gate near a clump of dark trees on your right. This is the entry to Peak Scar, a deep limestone gorge which boasts one of the "windy pits" which are a feature of this part of Ryedale. They do not, of course, compare with the huge caverns of Ingleton or Clapham, still less with those of the Pyrenees, but several generations of Ampleforth schoolboys have had great fun and not a little edification in digging up Stone Age relics from these caves.

Resuming your route from Peak Scar you continue along the narrow lane to the Hambleton Drove Road. The broad grass verges of this ancient way provided "bite" for the cattle making their way to southern markets where Scotch beef was appreciated long before Scotch whisky was heard of. This road is known by a different

Sutton Bank (Bernard Fearnley)

name in almost every parish through which it passes. Cleveland Road, Hambleton Road, Limekilns Road and High Street I can easily understand. Even Sneck Yat I can make a guess at. But the devil himself cannot tell why a stretch of this road should be called Lord's Tongue. Turn south along the Drove Road and soon you find yourself crossing the broad, open downlands where the hopes of the North are galloped. The pasture here is not so lush nor the air so tender to two-year-olds as in the Emerald Isle, but the Hambleton stables turn out some tough and hardy types. I take off my hat, for instance, to that ever-young, 12 year-old sprinter, Merry-Go-Round, who had his number in the frame more often than many an Irish horse made an appearance.

Beyond the gallops you come to Sutton Bank (see also page 29); here you turn left and follow the A170 towards Helmsley. If the traffic is not too heavy you can pause to take in the magnificent views across the Plain of York to the far Pennines. But if the traffic is fast and furious, follow the example of many others and park in the National Park's official car park. Don't however, follow the example of those who also park their "empties" there — cans, bottles or boxes! Do make use of the facilities offered at the Information Centre. The maps are particularly helpful if you wish to explore the area. There are two Nature Trails, organised by the Forestry Commission and the Yorkshire Naturalists. The second of these, down through Garbutt Wood to Gormire, should certainly not be missed.

Keep along the A170 to Sproxton and then turn down right, along the B1257 towards Malton. The next few miles are high on my list of favourite drives. First there is the broad upward sweep towards Oswaldkirk with the tall woods on the right and the sunlit valley below on the left. Then the road follows the centre of a low ridge with the most glorious panorama right ahead of the driver. This, of course, makes for safe driving as no one gets too near to the car in front lest it spoil the view. Hovingham is famous for its associations with a contemporary princess; this is in keeping with most ancient tradition for the higher tumulus just beyond the village is undoubtedly the tombstone of some Ancient British chieftainess, although certainly not Boadicea.

Two miles beyond is Slingsby. Turn left down to this village which is celebrated among the cognoscenti for the extra whiteness of its limestone cottages and the extra brightness of its red pantiled roofs. The stylish dignity of its two-storeyed, dormer windowed cottages adds to the attractions of this village, which is enhanced by the classic beauty of its Early English church. But the strangest and most noticeable feature of Slingsby is the House that Never Was. It lies on the left, half hidden in a wilderness of alder and fruit trees. It looks at first like the ruin on some mitred abbot's palace stripped of its leaden roof and stained glass. Tradition holds that some wealthy cavalier began it, a Cavendish perhaps. Then came the Civil War and the family fortunes were lost in the cause of Charles the Martyr. The restoration of the Merry Monarch, Charles II, brought no joy to our Slingsby cavalier for his great house remained unfinished as we see it today.

And so back across the chequered Vale of Pickering, crossing the Riccal, the Rye, the Dove and many parallel streams on their way to join the Derwent near Malton. Turn right along the A170 to Kirby Mills where you leave it to climb up beyond Hutton-le-Hole to Blakey Rigg between Farndale and Rosedale. You can take the narrow road, with a water splash, back to Teesside by Westerdale, Hob Hole and Kildale. Otherwise, use the wider but more roundabout route via Castleton and Lockwood Beck and the A171 Guisborough-Whitby road.

Teesside-Egton-Goathland-Low Dalby-Forest Drive - Hackness - West Ayton - Helmsley - Teesside

THIS run combines a pleasant moorland trip with a visit to the famous Forest Drive through Low Dalby to Hackness. This smooth tarmac road with lay-bys and picnic spots is not shown on any map in normal use though it is given prominence in the excellent little guide book "North Yorkshire Forests", published by HM Stationery Office. There are only a few places on this woodland way where passing of on-coming traffic is difficult, and with a little caution there should be no difficulty.

We leave Teesside by the A171 and we turn off to the right for Egton just beyond the milepost and the AA box 14 miles from Guisborough. Drop down through Egton village to cross the narrow bridge at a right angle bend and take the first left turn signposted to Goathland. Opposite the Mallyan Spout Hotel as you enter Goathland, turn right along an unfenced road to reach the A169 just above the Eller Beck Bridge, above which no doubt you will see the Fylingdale's "golf balls". Continue south taking a look at the Hole of Horcum on your right if you are new to this road. Take the first fork to the left at the Fox and Rabbit Inn, signposted Thornton Dale.

Old cross at Goathland (John Parker)

Two miles along this road look out for a fingerpost Low Dalby. As you enter this narrow lane, on the left you will see a much more elaborate notice board indicating that you are now on the "Forest Drive" through Hackness to Scarborough. These helpful signboards will take you 14 miles or so to Hackness along a road carefully planned by the Forestry Commission to offer viewpoints and picnic facilities to visitors. The first village you reach after about three miles is Low Dalby, one of the most attractive and well-designed homesteads one could wish to meet. It is a real tribute to careful siting and to the consideration which the forestry and the county planning officers have shown to the preservation of amenity. To those who have the inclination to leave their cars and take a stroll, signposts indicate other places of interest such as the High Bride Stones on National Trust property just to the north of Staindale on Lockton Moor.

In Hackness, take the right turn to West Ayton. This takes you through Forge Valley, a noted beauty spot which will be looking particularly lovely when the trees begin to change their colour. Return to Teesside via the A170 as far as Helmsley where you cross the market square to take the right turning B1257 through Bilsdale and Stokesley. This is, of course, the most direct and easily found route. Some may prefer to use the higher roads over Blakey Rigg and Rosedale Rigg, which we have used in earlier runs.

Saltburn - Danby - Glaisdale - Hole of Horcum - Pickering - Newton - Cropton - Hutton-le-Hole - Westerdale - Saltburn

THE road pattern of our local dales was not designed for fast through traffic. In fact it has hardly changed since the eighteenth century. There are ridge roads with never a hamlet for miles on end. They converge on a central village or market town. Below the ridge roads lie the farmsteads, each with its outlet to the ridge road. Occasionally the farms on one side of a valley are linked by a narrow lane or a roughly paved field road; more rarely is there a cross-dale road linking the two sides of a valley. The result for motorists can be terribly frustrating or utterly delightful according to mood or intention.

I find a run along the Esk valley fits far oftener into the second category, especially if someone else is driving. There is much low gear work on bends and hills. There are pauses at the dozens of intersections. This, for me, is the ideal way of learning to know the countryside. The very mode of travel itself forces one to look around and observe closely. But wandering aimlessly around Eskdale, or any other dale for that matter, while being interesting, can be annoying and even expensive. To glide gently between hedge-rows of honeysuckle or briar only to find your delightful country lane ends at an old barn or a disused quarry is bad enough. But when you try to reverse and rip your exhause pipe or number plate on a stone hidden in the long grass of the verge, you can only sigh with the psalmist, "My cup runneth over".

I started my run from Saltburn and went up to Skelton along the B1268 and B1267 to reach the A173. This I duly turned off up to Lingdale and Lockwood Beck where I joined the caravanserai to the coast along the moor road (A171). Three miles on, right at the top of the moor, I took the sharp right turn for Danby. This point gives perhaps the finest view of the broadest stretch of heather moor that one is likely to see. As you enter Danby village, slow down to be ready to take the left turn at the Duke of Wellington. The next fork is to the right, again at the foot of a sharp descent, with a glimpse of the tall trimmed hedges of Danby Lodge which is now a well-equipped information centre.

Under the railway bridge fork left (unless you wish to stop and have a look at the famous Duck Bridge or wander up to Danby

St. Cedd's Well, Lastingham
(Alec Wright)

Castle). Another mile to another fork, this time to the right for Fryup. You cross the Esk and run in a gentle switchback for about a mile. Avoid two right turns up into Fryup, but take the third turn right to Glaisdale at the top of a rise just beyond Wheat Bank Farm. This drops down across Busco Beck and enters Glaisdale where you follow the main road in a half circle from the church down to cross the Esk near the picturesque Beggars' Bridge. Up Limber Hill you go, having, I hope, replaced any L driver who may have been giving father a rest. At a bend just after the road flattens out, turn sharply down to Egton Bridge, a tortuous climb and steep drop amply rewarded by a superbly beautiful stretch of road close to the Esk. Up to the left to Egton village and then sharp right turn down to Grosmont, where the right fork above the village leads to the A169 to Pickering.

There are the usual distractions here for the driver—the parked cars above Eller Beck waiting to feed the Lyke Wake walkers, the imposing but incongruous "golf balls" at Fylingdales and the snowstorm of toffee papers and lolly covers near the Hole of Horcum car park. I can thoroughly recommend a diversion to Lockton and Levisham, two miles south of the Hole of Horcum. These villages are picturesque and their inns hospitable. The greens offer parking space and there are exciting glacial valleys to explore to the north and west if you care to get out of the car and walk half a mile or so. Rejoin the A169 and as you enter Pickering fork right to the station and at the level crossing take a delightful riverside road up to Newton Rawcliffe, one of the few villages which still retains a wide pond in a spacious green.

Once again in this, the Vale of Pickering, you resume the switchback you experienced in Eskdale. Turning left at the top of Newton, you fork left again when the road turns up north for Stape. If it is evening, and your tank needs a refill, go down to Wrelton from Cropton, as there are not many filling stations open in the villages of the foothills. Otherwise turn right in Cropton for Lastingham, and almost immediately left again at a little stream, where the right fork goes up into Rosedale.

Lastingham deserves a longer stay than we have time for on this occasion, so turn to your right in the village for Hutton-le-Hole by the streamside road. Turn sharp right once again as you enter the top of Hutton-le-Hole village and follow the Blakey Rigg road to the Lion Inn. If you want a sandwich here you may have to wait a minute or so. They are busy on a Sunday night! But at least the sandwiches are fresh. If you take the left fork just over a mile beyond the Lion, you will find the Westerdale - Hob-Hole - Kildale - Guisborough road far less crowded than the Castleton - Lockwood Beck road and the A171 down Birk Brow. Return to Saltburn via Upleatham.

Teesside - Commondale - Westerdale - Kirkbymoorside - Hovingham - Ampleforth - White Horse - Teesside

I NEED no computerised statistics to convince me that far more visitors reach Kilburn's White Horse from West Yorkshire than from Teesside. Car number plates and voices are sufficient evidence of this western invasion of one of the most sheltered and attractive sections of the North York Moors National Park, in the lee of the Hambleton Hills. In fact, many consider Oldstead to be in the most sheltered situation in Yorkshire. There is no denying this connection. Oldstead lies some two miles from Byland Abbey up the little valley of Cockerdale which is immune to every breeze that blows and catches all the sun.

This run will take us along this winding road below the southern arm of the Hambleton Hills and we will approach our day's target by a route through Kildale and Farndale to get a scent of the heather and a look at the harvest from some superb viewpoints. From the west end of Ayton, cross the Leven and take the signpost to Easby and Kildale. Through Kildale you continue to Commondale. There is a curious guidestone on the left of the road just above Commondale: it is one of several "handstones" carved by some signwriter who had obviously a very crude idea of human anatomy.

Go up to the White Cross junction and turn right along the road for Castleton. At the bridge beyond Castleton railway station turn right for Westerdale. There are a number of crossroads hereabouts and wayfinding is not particularly easy, but if you keep parallel with the stream below you and keep a careful eye on the signposts you should not go far astray. From Westerdale make due south for the moor top. Follow the high ridge road south to the Lion Inn and about half a mile further on take the right fork down into Farndale.

At the foot of the steep bank take the left fork and follow the "East Side" road and the signposts to Gillamoor. This will bring you in a half circle to Low Mills where there is a large car park for those who want a streamside stroll. Our trip continues along the signposted road up the hillside from Low Mills towards Gillamoor and Kirkbymoorside. It is on this stretch of road that there are two or three really exceptional viewpoints.

After dropping down through Kirkbymoorside's long market street to the A170 you turn right for about two miles and then take the left turn beyond a handsome lodge gate at Welburn. Take the first right (signpost Nunnington and Wombleton) and follow

Cottages at Great Ayton (Keith Robson)

the signposts through Nunnington towards Hovingham. Note the avenues of oak trees through which this road runs. As you drop down the bank beyond Nunnington you turn right along the B1257 to Helmsley and about three miles on fork very sharp left (B1363) on the Gilling road.

You leave the B1363 almost immediately and fork right through Oswaldkirk whose cottages seem almost to be suspended from the wooded face of the steep hillside—the church on the right will certainly come as something of a surprise in this old world setting. You are now on the picturesque run that is so deservedly popular with the West Yorkshire visitors: Ampleforth, Wass, Byland Abbey, Oldstead and on towards Kilburn, following the signposts. A mile and a half beyond Oldstead, almost immediately below the White Horse, a narrow road climbs steeply up to the right and there is a fair-sized car park half way up the hill. To get back to Teesside, keep on uphill. The narrow road passes the glider station. Turn right on reaching the A170 and then after about a mile and a half follow the signpost on the left to Scawton and Rievaulx, beyond which you come home along Bilsdale and the B1257.

Whitby - Ugthorpe - Grosmont - Sleights - Littlebeck - Whitby

THIS is virtually a run from Whitby—but it is obviously also quite accessible for an afternoon or evening outing from any point between Staithes and Scarborough. I have one warning! There are so many unusually decorative houses and gardens along these twisting roads that your womenfolk will be nudging you to a halt at almost every bend in the road. I can visualise some frustrated drivers in the Sleights area if it is fine.

We will start from Lythe village on the A174 and take the road south from the village square to Ugthorpe. This stretch of lane has fascinating glimpses of the spacious valley around Mulgrave Woods. The road winds up and down through delightful shady dells and patches of sun-chequered woodland.

In one of these steep-sided valleys there is a crossroads and your route lies straight ahead, although straight can hardly be the appropriate word. You strike the A171 about a mile beyond the rather austere village of Ugthorpe and turn left towards Whitby. Just below the AA box take the right fork to Egton and then take the left turn near the end of the village green to Grosmont.

As you drop down the narrow road to Grosmont you cannot but be impressed with the glorious situation of this village, strung out along the southern slopes of Eskdale. Red and blue-grey roofs peep out from the treetops, nestling under the dominant curiously-coloured church like chicks under the wings of a fat old Sussex hen. The charm of Grosmont was always marred for me by the industrial terraced cottages at the western approaches. Some of these are in the process of demolition, so one can say that Grosmont is now one of the most unspoiled of all our dales villages. This remains true in spite of the holiday crowds which throng the village now that the railway to Pickering has been reopened by the North York Moors Historical Railway Trust. The railway is by far the best means of access to the long narrow valley with its old deciduous woods and its except -ional rock formations. There are car parks provided by both the National Parks and by the railway.

You follow the signposted switchback road to Sleights where you turn left down the A169 for a few yards, but almost immediately right again at the war memorial—the signpost is Sneaton and Uggle-barnby. For the curious, this placename means the "farm of Old Owl

The roofs of Whitby (Albert Walker)

Beard". As you climb up from the bridge at Iburndale take the fork to the right and at the T-junction a mile farther on take the right turn once again for Littlebeck. Any readers who may have set out from Robin Hood's Bay or Scarborough could start their circular tour at this point which is just below the B1416 linking Scarborough and Ruswarp. Notice the drinking fountain just beyond the tiny hamlet of Hempsyke — you cannot fail to be struck by the Victorian sentimentality of the verses engraved — but I prefer the tramp to the self-styled poet, who very obviously fancied himself a little too much.

If you are in the middle of a weekend convoy you will find it almost impossible to stop in the narrow twisting road through Littlebeck. Here is a dream village if ever there was one. I saw it at its best in the calm of a late evening when the sun gave an extra coat of gilt to the rose gardens around the Mill House. Above Littlebeck the narrow lane swings sharp right parallel with the stream for about a mile. Then it forks suddenly up to the left to come out on the A169 just above Sleights.

This road strikes the main Whitby-Guisborough road three miles ahead and readers will seek their tents, homes or caravan sites as they choose. For those who want to complete the circular tour from Lythe, a pleasant route is found by taking the A171 for one mile to the west from the junction with the Sleights road (A169). Then turn right, down the narrow road to Newholme to reach the coast road (A174) at Whitby golf course. Turn left for Sandsend and Lythe.

Helmsley - Bransdale - Fadmoor - Kirkdale - Helmsley

THE dales of the North York Moors National Park, whether their streams flow into the Rye or the Esk, are much of a pattern. Those who have joined "the Sunday circular" to see the Farndale daffodils will recognise it. A road runs along the west side—from Low Mills. It crosses the floor of the valley to Church Houses and comes back along the east side of the dale to swing up to the ridge road. There are few dales indeed where this system of the "parish road" linking the farms along each side of the valley is not found. Bilsdale is, of course, a notable exception. It is the one valley which has a through road, running fairly close to the main stream. The B1257 from Stokesley is almost the only convenient link between Teesside and Ryedale.

From Helmsley market place take the A170 to the end of the street and turn left to Carlton. You climb steadily up this white road amid the walled fields so typical of this limestone country. A mile beyond Carlton you suddenly find the countryside opening out in front of you, almost exploding. This "surprise view" is found as you approach nearly all these valleys from the south. You climb gradually on the long gentle southern slopes and then find yourself with a precipitous drop into a different world. Miles and miles of dark heather moor, hardly a house to be seen, scarcely a tree, as the moorlands stretch onwards and upwards to the Cleveland escarpment a dozen miles or more to the north.

This is an excellent point to stop for a look round. There are forestry rides in all directions and pedestrians are welcome, particularly non-smokers. Bracken can be tinder dry: a light spark could cause a serious forest fire. The dale below is Riccaldale, a naturalist's paradise, although picnic parties must be wary of the huge ants' nests which abound here. If you decide to go further, follow the narrow road across the dale: look out for the tiny church of Lund in the trees behind the phone box on your right. What a marvellous setting!

Keep steadily climbing north. Slowly please! There are young lambs about. Two miles of barren heather-clad moor bring you to a green oasis around one of the loneliest farmhouses in Yorkshire— Bonfield (Bonny Field?) Gill. The road (there is only one) crosses this gill and once again winds its narrow way through the heather, drops into the broad head of Bransdale and crosses the valley floor before winding its way up to the ridge road to Kirkbymoorside on the east side of the dale. The road is unfenced once you leave the cultivated fields on the lower slopes of Bransdale. There are splendid views of the Hodge Beck on your right and the escarpment of the Tabular Hills away to the east.

You reach a signposted crossroads at a point on Rudland Rigg: the signpost indicates Stokesley 16 miles. This road is very rough, as you can see. Climbing down to Battersby at the northern end would be even rougher. I do not recommend it, but quite a few cars do attempt it. You must, therefore, turn right to Kirkbymoorside and take a right fork two miles farther on to Fadmoor. At the end of this hamlet, fork right once more. The signpost says Welburn and Sleightholme Dale. Turn sharp left at the next fork. Two miles farther south turn sharp right for Kirkdale. Take the ford steadily, it is sometimes deeper than you think. Then climb steadily—you are to turn unexpectedly sharp right to St. Gregory's Minster at the top of the hill.

I will not describe St. Gregory's ancient church except to say that it is in by far the most photogenic surroundings of any church I know. Its particular interest is, of course, the ancient sundial in the church porch, divided into Anglo-Saxon "tides", not hours. Alongside is an inscription that must be one of the earliest pieces of English still extant. The Minster is a mile from the A170 whether you turn right or go straight on at the first fork. A further four miles ahead is Helmsley.